"Jonathan and Andi Goldman have written an intriguing book that focuses on the use of energy and vibration to shift consciousness, and how these elements can bring greater harmony and creativity to relationships. Whether you're in a close relationship now or aspire to bring one into your life, you will reap real benefits from reading *Tantra of Sound.*"

—Gay and Kathlyn Hendricks, co-authors of *Conscious Loving* and *Lasting Love*

"Powerful! . . . Timely! *The Tantra of Sound* leads us into a journey to the core of our most basic needs, and deepest beliefs. Through a rare fusion of timeless wisdom and spirituality, Jonathan and Andi Goldman describe how the healing power of sound unlocks the mystery of our most intimate relationships. In doing so they open the door to a new genre of emotional tantra, and spiritual mastery. *The Tantra of Sound* is essential to the library of anyone on the 'Path!'"

—Gregg Braden, author of *The God Code* and *The Isaiah Effect*

Other books by Jonathan Goldman:
Healing Sounds
Shifting Frequencies
The Lost Chord

TANTRA

OF

SOUND

how to enhance intimacy with sound

Jonathan Goldman

and

Andi Goldman

HAMPTON ROADS
PUBLISHING COMPANY, INC.

Cover design by Grace Pedalino
Cover digital imagery © 2004 Creatas/Thinkstock

Hampton Roads Publishing Company, Inc.
1125 Stoney Ridge Road
Charlottesville, VA 22902

434-296-2772
fax: 434-296-5096
e-mail: hrpc@hrpub.com
www.hrpub.com

If you are unable to order this book from your local
bookseller, you may order directly from the publisher.
Call 1-800-766-8009, toll-free.

Library of Congress Cataloging-in-Publication Data

Goldman, Jonathan, 1949-
Tantra of sound : how to enhance intimacy / Jonathan Goldman and Andi
Goldman.
p. cm.
Summary: "A guide to using sound as a way to enhance intimacy in
relationships and increase awareness in all aspects of life. Includes guided
meditations and toning and breathing exercises to activate the chakras.
Includes a music CD to be used in conjunction with the book and
exercises"--Provided by publisher.
Includes index.
ISBN 1-57174-432-0 (alk. paper)
1. Intimacy (Psychology) 2. Sound--Therapeutic use. 3. Medicine, Magic,
mystic, and spagiric. I. Goldman, Andi, 1948- II. Title.
HQ801.G5873 2005
158.2--dc22
2004024313

10 9 8 7 6 5 4 3 2 1
Printed on acid-free paper in the United States

Dedication

Tantra of Sound has been a work of love. We dedicate this book to each other. Neither one of us could have done it without the other. We are grateful for our love, our companionship, and our extraordinary commitment to work together for personal and planetary healing.

We dedicate this to our families: to our son Joshua; to our parents, Rose and Irving Goldman and Andrew and Bettye Pullman; our brothers and sisters, Richard and Peter Goldman, Richard Pullman, and Suzanne Strauss.

We would like to acknowledge and dedicate this book to some of the people whose work, support, and essence have allowed us to manifest this book. Some of these people are not on the planet, but their work continues to resonate and affect us. Others are here, without knowledge of this book, although their work and energy have inspired and taught us. Others are colleagues, friends, and loved ones who have been there with us through the birthing of this creation. These people include Jim Albani, Chris Allen, Kimba Arem, John

Beaulieu, Sarah Benson and Donald Beaman, PJ Birosik and Paul Scott, Steve Brown, Gregg Braden, Don Campbell, Deepak Chopra, Roberta Collier-Morales, Tae Darnell, Vickie Dodd and Eric Neurath, Dan Furst, John and Ali Galm, Kay Gardner, Steven Halpern, Gay and Kathlyn Hendricks, Nan Kenney, Kitaro, Keiko, Lama Tashi, Laraaji, Reb. Auri V. Ishi, Randall McClellan, Meredith McCord, Mary Magdalena, Kay Mora, David and Laurie Rugenstein, Reb. Zalman Schachter-Shalomi, Jill Schumacher, Ed and Deb Shapiro, Alec Sims, and Patricia Youngson. Special thanks to Frank DeMarco for his expert editorial support, compassion, and wisdom.

In addition, we wish to give our heartfelt gratitude for the guidance, wisdom, and compassion of all the extraordinary energies and divine beings who work with us and through us.

Finally, with loving kindness, we acknowledge and dedicate this book to you, dear reader. May these words assist in manifesting beneficial shifts and changes in you and all those you touch. We send Blessings of Light and Love through Sound to all who pass through these pages.

Contents

Part IV. Other Applications

Appendices

Introduction

Welcome to *Tantra of Sound*! You are about to embark on an exciting journey using the power of sound as a tool for enhancing your life. It will open doors of intimacy not only with yourself but also with your partner, whether lover, friend, spouse, or other. Although in our Western culture tantra is most often associated with sex, you will discover that *Tantra of Sound* is an exploration of sound as a vehicle for self-awareness, allowing you to discover a new and exciting paradigm for raising consciousness and enhancing all areas of your life.

As a couple and in working with thousands of people in our seminars, we have successfully used and applied the knowledge and exercises we now present to you. Everything in *Tantra of Sound* is true and works. Its simple yet effective information and techniques can change your life. Sound can be an extraordinary teacher, showing you how to achieve states of consciousness not normally available to those uninitiated to its power. Through sound it is possible to be healed and made whole, and to awaken your consciousness to tantra, the web of existence that connects everything. This is the power of *Tantra of Sound* and why we have written it for you.

Sound can heal the body, mind, and spirit, as well as the emotions. Through this interrelationship of sound and self, we can balance and harmonize any of these aspects within ourselves and affect all parts of our being. Through this resonance with sound, we can heal our inner self, as well as create harmony within our relationships. Once this powerful new awareness of self emerges, we begin to experience life differently; we are open to the possibilities inherent in the human experience.

Tantra of Sound is based on more than 40 years of our combined experience working in the fields of sound, health, and consciousness. To our knowledge, no one has ever brought together the information and techniques found within these pages in such a framework as this. Our unique and powerful approach of using sound to enhance intimacy and relationship is new and innovative. It is also extremely effective.

One of the main purposes of this book is to create a vehicle for individuals or couples to use to deepen relationships, enhance more self-awareness, and create more love in their lives. Through the powerful exercises and techniques presented in this book you will learn to tune and vibrate your body, mind, and spirit through sound. When this harmony occurs, all is possible, including enhanced physical, emotional, mental, and spiritual balance and bonding. It will change your life.

Tantra of Sound is divided into four parts. The first section focuses on "Basic Principles" found in both tantra and sound. We answer questions such as "What is tantra?" and "How can sound assist the tantric experience?" You'll learn about tantra as the web that unites all reality and about sound as the fundamental vibratory force. You'll discover how sound has the ability to shift and change us. You'll find out how this energy can be applied individually or with couples to enhance well-being and intimacy with self and others. You'll explore aspects of vibration that include resonance, intention, entrainment, visualization, and many other fascinating aspects of sound and consciousness.

In the second part of this book we delve into "Basic Practices" for using sound as a vehicle to promote intimacy by balancing the energy centers known as chakras. Included in this section is the important use of breath and toning in order to begin utilizing your voice for self-created sounds. You'll learn exercises using sacred vowel sounds and mantras to affect and align your nervous system and your chakras. You'll begin to experience the power of your own resonance as you explore the innermost aspects of yourself through the power of sound. You will lay the groundwork for feeling confident about exploring tantric sound practices with a partner.

The third part of *Tantra of Sound* involves the use of sound as a tool to exchange energy with another person. This section, called "Practice with a Partner," is designed for you to experience specific sound exercises with another in order to deepen your relationship. You'll also be asking yourself important questions concerning your purpose for using sound with a partner. You'll then explore profound and powerful techniques to use with a partner. These will greatly assist and enhance all aspects of relationship.

The fourth section of this book, "Other Applications," examines additional uses and areas for using sound to enrich your life. We introduce new sounds and new ways to use them that will create a happier, healthier you, including how music can be used to initiate different states of consciousness and enhance your life experiences. We look at many other ways in which sound can assist your well-being.

We've also included appendices, with information on sonic tools such as tuning forks and crystal bowls, recommended recordings and books, and further commentary on sound.

To truly know oneself is to begin to catch a glimpse of the Divine. We have forgotten our connection to who and what we are. Because of this, many of us find our lives have lost meaning. Sound is a major key to rediscovering this knowing of self. We can use sound to reconnect, strengthen, and revitalize our lives.

Sound is a dynamic agent for shift and change. Knowledge of sound can enhance practically any activity you engage in. It can change your life. *Tantra of Sound* has chapters on experiencing sound exercises individually as well as with a partner. The potential uses of sound for change are limitless.

Imagine you're feeling depressed, with low energy and no vigor. Your passion for life seems to have slipped away. You start working with sound and suddenly, within a few minutes, your depression begins to lift and your life energy returns. Or perhaps you're with your partner and not feeling connected with each other or the least bit romantic. In fact, you're having a good old-fashioned emotional battle that has both of you ready to give up the relationship. What if you could both "sound" together and, within a few minutes, be back to a place where you are talking to each other again, perhaps even beginning to resonate with the love that you have? What if you found that by working with sound for just a short amount of time each day, you could heal many different issues, allowing you a life of balance and happiness?

We know that this and more can be achieved through *Tantra of Sound*—that learning to understand and use sound in an intimate and sacred manner can lead to all sorts of extraordinary realizations about yourself, your relationships, and your life. Sound has been a wonderful teacher for us; it has helped us in our loving resonance with each other, and we know it can help you.

Tantra of Sound is the result of an act of love—not only for each other but also for our planet. We like to think that it combines the best of our talents, abilities, and gifts. And that, in the end, the love we are able to give to each other, and ultimately to you, the reader, is a direct result of the love we are able to receive from each other.

Before we begin this extraordinary journey into sound and intimacy, we would like to thank you in advance for joining us and for allowing us to share our journey with you. We know it will change your life.

We send many Blessings of Light and Love through Sound to you on this journey!

Andi and Jonathan Goldman

Boulder, Colorado 2004

Part I

Basic Principles

What Is Tantra of Sound?

Tantra. The very word conjures up exciting images of incense-filled rooms, full of throbbing bodies pulsating and vibrating in various degrees of orgasmic ecstasy. Indeed, if you do an Internet search on the word "tantra," you will find over a million and a half websites with reference to that word. Almost all of these sites focus on sex. Sex is huge. Sex sells. To many people, sex and tantra mean the same thing. This, however, is simply not true.

There is great confusion today about the word "tantra," and understandably so. Depending on the culture, tradition, viewpoint, teacher, and level of awareness, tantra means different things to different people. In our research for this book, we investigated numerous sources and were astounded by the variety of meanings that were applied to the word and the teachings behind it.

Not surprisingly, here in the West, the meaning of tantra is almost always synonymous with sex and sexual yoga, taken from specific paths and teachers in the Hindu tradition. Yet in the Buddhist tradition, particularly Tibetan Buddhism, tantra has nothing to do with sex—at least not with the physical aspect of sexual relationships.

As noted, an Internet search on the word "tantra" reveals over a million and a half websites addressing aspects of tantra, the vast majority of which center on sex. In our own search, an estimated 90 percent to 95 percent of the sites we visited involved some aspect of sexual relations—with everything from sexual aids to sexual surrogates being advertised. Many times these sites offered techniques for improving sexual capability in sexual relationships. Many times, however, these sites were not nearly that subtle.

Yet in our research we also discovered sources that were of seemingly pure tantric traditions, and they were almost all adamant that tantra has little or nothing to do with sex as it is currently perceived in the West. In fact, the word "neo-tantra" frequently emerged when authorities on traditional tantra dealt with the subject of this newer Western perception of tantra as sex, which they considered a corruption of true tantra. What, then, is tantra?

The Meaning of Tantra

Tantra is Sanskrit, the ancient language of the Hindu tradition. As in other sacred languages such as Hebrew or Tibetan, there is frequently no one single meaning that can be applied in translation. Thus *tantra* is often translated as "continuum" or "unbroken stream" and indicates a flow of consciousness from ignorance to enlightenment. The word also translates as "web" or "warp" and encompasses all that is. Tantra represents the interconnecting energies between all things in this and other planes of existence. Other words used to describe tantra are: leading principle, essential part, model, system, framework, doctrine, rule, theory, scientific work, order, chief part, rule, authority, science, mystic works, magical formulas, means, expedient, stratagem, and medicine.

The etymology of *tantra* points to the combination of two words, *tattva* and *mantra*. Tattva is the science of cosmic principles, while mantra refers to the science of mystic sound and vibrations. In the Tibetan Buddhist tradition, tantra is sometimes referred to as "Secret Mantra." This may be to distinguish it from Western concepts of neo-tantra. A definition of "Secret Mantra" from the Tibetan Buddhist standpoint is as follows: "Secret" indicates that these methods should be practiced privately; "mantra" means "protection for the mind" and often utilizes sacred sound to provide this. Thus the function of Secret Mantra is to enable us through the use of sound to progress swiftly through the stages of the spiritual path by protecting our mind against ordinary conceptions.

Indeed, one of the highest levels of tantric practice involves resonating and harmonizing oneself with sound. This is done in order to enhance and energize our physical, mental, emotional, and spiritual essences. Hindu and Tibetan Buddhist tantra both stress the power of sound. Sound, in fact, is the basis of much tantra—through working with advanced sound techniques, tantric practitioners are able to harmonize themselves in body, mind, and spirit.

It was through our work exploring various sonic practices from the Eastern traditions that we came upon the concept of *Tantra of Sound*. Through years of using sound, we have discovered easy methods for achieving the harmonizing effect that Eastern mystics have described. This desired harmony and balance of body, mind, and spirit can be both safely and efficiently achieved by the reader utilizing the techniques and exercises described in this book.

As we will discuss throughout the book, our primary goal is to assist the reader in reaching deeper states of consciousness and awareness; first with yourself, and then, if appropriate, with a partner. Humanity is currently at a crossroads in its evolutionary development. One road leads to an amazing new world of hopes and possibilities filled with love and compassion, caring and kindness. The other road does not. This first road offers the potential for us to become the true, extraordinary humans that so many of the mystics and spiritual teachers throughout time have suggested that we can be. In order to do so, we must achieve harmony and balance within ourselves and then with one another. We must be willing to gaze into the window of our soul, acknowledge who and what we are, and then agree to love and honor that being.

At this crossroads, a time when various spiritual traditions from the Mayan to the Christian have foretold great change, we find that different models or archetypes must emerge. The current paradigm that we have dealt with in our psyche, and have manifested in the physical for many thousands of years, has resulted in war and suffering. We suggest it is possible to choose a different model based on harmony, balance, cooperation, and compassion. This model exists in the various myths, legends, and spiritual texts of the planet and represents both strength and goodness. It is not necessary to be weak in order to be kind; currently, we often confuse and equate these two.

The model we present in *Tantra of Sound* is one that is balanced and aligned with the harmonious integration of the masculine and feminine energies within each person. When these energies are embodied, they create an egalitarian relationship with the self and others. This relationship is not controlling nor is it in competition with the participants involved. It is cooperative and compassionate. It is balanced and harmonious.

Balanced relationships have manifested through many of the divine beings in different cultures who generate loving-kindness, from Shiva and Shakti in the Hindu tradition to Avalokitesvara and Tara in the Tibetan Buddhist tradition, and to Jesus and Mary Magdalene in the Christian tradition. These energies may be understood as being divine entities and their consorts, or as a priest and high priestess who work together in the sacred loving unity of the Divine. These male and female energies are found within us individually and are created through partnership. We are not talking about gender separation but rather about the balanced energies of the internalized masculine and feminine.

The uniting of masculine and feminine energies is found in

tantra, which utilizes the symbolic male/female union within as a meditative form to assist in achieving enlightenment. A tantric practitioner concentrates on expanding all levels of consciousness in order to unveil and experience the supreme reality of God. This is done through symbolically uniting the two opposite energies of the male and female (in Hinduism, the Shiva-Shakti energy). Through tantra, one can overcome the maya or illusion of separateness, which manifests in lower levels of consciousness that create the polarity of male and female. True reality equals the Absolute, and that is non-dualistic. It encompasses the unification of the masculine and feminine aspects within us so that we may transcend into the oneness of the Divine.

We believe that this paradigm of harmonious and balanced male/female energy is necessary for our continued journey down the evolutionary road. We have reached the place in our development where the use of our technology must be tempered with the wisdom of loving-kindness. We offer you *Tantra of Sound* to assist in the integration of this important paradigm of relationship for the benefit of both personal and planetary acceleration.

The Web of Life

From our perspective, tantra is the web that interconnects and unites all of reality. Modern science is beginning to acknowledge this interconnectedness—that we are all part of one huge matrix of consciousness. Indeed, quantum physics tells us that the observer and the system observed form an inseparable whole. Everything is interrelated. One object or experience is not separate from another. Experiments have demonstrated nonlocality, showing that simultaneous events far removed geographically from each other can indeed influence and affect each other. Thus it is said that the beating of the wings of a butterfly over Kansas can affect the weather patterns over Europe.

Nearly one hundred years ago, noted psychologist Carl Jung

coined the term "synchronicity" to describe how two apparently unrelated events could be related. He noted that there is more to life's seemingly "accidental" events than just coincidence. Jung talked about a collective unconscious—a unified field of thought.

We are all interrelated and not so alone and isolated from each other as we may believe. The study of tantra incorporates this understanding of all things being interrelated. Tantra tells us not only that all things are connected, but also that all things are part of the One—the Divine, the supreme universal mind, or the God Force.

Many of us feel isolated and detached in our lives. We feel separate from each other, separate from ourselves, and separate from the Divine. This is a commonplace experience for many people. Our consciousness of duality—that things are disconnected from each other—creates this separateness that we experience. Understanding tantra provides for the realization of the One—transcending duality and providing a consciousness of unity that acknowledges the divinity in all.

Using Sound to Unite

As you will soon discover, sound is an extraordinary vehicle to unite and to assist us in the dissolution of our sense of separation, creating unification through vibratory resonance. Through sound, we can unify ourselves, experiencing a nondualistic reality that allows us to resonate with the oneness of the Divine.

We have found that focusing on sound provides a fast and effective means for Westerners to work with the higher levels of tantra, creating that deeper relationship with oneself and, if appropriate, with others. As we mentioned in the introduction, through utilizing sound in this manner we can achieve a powerful and deep understanding of ourselves, as well as others. Such powerful intimacy, created through the power of sound and acted on with the power of love, can only enhance our lives—assisting our health and wellness and leading to an eventual resonance of harmony and balance with the web of life. This is tantra of sound.

It is not necessary to have a partner in order to experience tantra. In Tibetan Buddhism, tantra is normally practiced alone, uniting the divine forces as one within you. Traditionally, a tantric practitioner's meditations incorporate the visualizations of male and female deities. Tantra is understood as a path that allows the transmutation of imbalanced energies, enabling one to overcome suffering and ultimately enter nirvana, the heavenly realms. It is a path of enlightenment, which utilizes the energy of compassion through sound.

Much of this understanding is also true in the tantra of the Hindu tradition. The universe is considered the cosmic interplay of male/female energy. The whole process of creation, preservation, and destruction is the manifestation of this male/female energy—the dance of Shiva/Shakti. The existence of the world is thought of as a continuous birthing of the female principle created from an infinite infusion of the male principle in sexual union. The universe—the web—is viewed as the act of ongoing creation expressed by patterns of symbolic sexual activity, suffused with a sense of transcendent love.

It is from the Hindu tradition that sex as a physical activity has come into our awareness as being synonymous with tantra. Yet, in actuality, many true Hindu tantric practitioners are celibate, focusing, like their Tibetan Buddhist counterparts, on the *symbolic union* of male/female energy. This union of the male/female energy—the Shiva-Shakti current—is metaphoric, ritualistic, and meditational. It is only a specific variation of Hindu tantra that actually works with physical sex between partners. This is the left-hand path of tantra, known as Vamacara, which has become the focus of much Western awareness of tantra.

Despite their varying approaches, the tantra of Tibetan Buddhism and that of Hinduism are extremely advanced practices that demand much work, study, and technical experience before their true benefits of enlightenment may be achieved. Because of this, traditional tantric practices are not designed for dabblers in the esoteric arts. Most Westerners do not have the time or the inclination for the lifelong commitment required by traditional tantric practice. Many may also find these practices out of harmony with their current religious or spiritual belief systems. It is for these reasons and others that we created this book.

Our techniques and understanding of these processes, which enable this harmonization to be achieved, are based to some degree on the traditional teachings of both Hindu and Tibetan Buddhist tantra, including knowledge of mantras, visualization, and chakras. They are also based on other spiritual and mystical traditions that understand the principles of sound as a healing and transformational energy.

Our teachings and techniques also incorporate modern methodologies and modalities that allow an easy and effective sonic resonance to occur. These teachings synergize and synthesize for rapid and powerful results. In addition, these teachings do not require much adherence to the belief system inherent in Hinduism and Tibetan Buddhism. They can easily be applied to our Western consciousness. While the teachings can certainly work within perspectives of consciousness of the Hindu or Buddhist belief system, they are equally applicable to anyone, regardless of religious beliefs or spiritual understanding. Tantra of sound is universal.

Sound is the essence of tantra. As we stated previously, tantra is partially derived from the word "mantra," which refers to the science of mystic sound and vibration. Thus tantra of sound means using sound as a tool to experience the web of the universe. In particular, we will focus on using self-created sounds in order to do this.

For those unaccustomed to singing or using your voice as an instrument of sound, we assure you that it is not necessary to have any sort of musical skills or gifts in order to experience the benefits in this book. Everyone, including those without any previous musical talent or training, can do the exercises we offer. You will discover that we all have the extraordinary ability to use self-created sound as a transformational tool. One of our purposes in this book is to help empower you with the use of your own voice to create powerful shifts and changes within yourself and with others.

We are not promising instant enlightenment through use of the material in this book. We suggest, however, that this material provides information and knowledge, as well as exercises and techniques, which, when properly applied, can lead to a happier, healthier, more balanced life. *Tantra of Sound* will open you to a deeper connection with yourself, and through this connection a powerful inner knowing of the oneness of all will emerge. You will learn how to shift and change your own vibratory levels in order to adjust to the many personal and planetary shifts that are currently happening.

Stay with us now as we begin our next chapter on the energy of sound. As you do, you will begin to learn more about the power and wonder of sound. And you will begin to experience deep transformation and change.

⋑ 2 ⋐

In the Beginning:
The Power of Sound

Sound is the unifying aspect of tantra, the web that connects all existence. Sound is the source of all being; vibration is the basis of all our reality. If you examine the basic tenets of the various religions and mystical paths on this planet, they all have awareness that sound is the principal creative force in the universe. This knowledge and understanding seem to be prevalent in most of the ancient spiritual teachings and centers throughout the world including Rome, Athens, Egypt, Tibet, and many other Mystery schools. To the Tibetan Buddhist, for example, the world is not only created through sound, it is constantly being recreated every moment of every day through the combination of thoughts and sounds. With this understanding comes awareness of the power of sound to heal and transform.

In the New Testament, it is written: "In the Beginning was the Word and the Word was God." The Hindu holy books, the Vedas, state: "In the beginning was Brahman with whom was the Word and the Word was Brahman." From Genesis in the Old Testament, we are told Sound is the first creative act of God, preceding the manifestation of Light; it is the act of speaking that creates the energy of Light. "And the Lord said 'Let there be Light!' and there was Light!"

The Hopi legends tell the story of the Spider Woman who sang the song of creation over all the inanimate forms on the planet and brought them to life. From the Mayan holy book, Popol Vuh, the first men and women were created solely through the power of sound. In ancient Egypt, the god Thoth would think of an object, speak its name, and bring it into being. In the Hebrew mystical path of Kabbalah, an object and its true name are identical. In the East, gods and goddesses blow conch shells or hit giant gongs, bringing the universe into creation. Stories, legends, and myths about sound as the basic creative force are found in all the countries and cultures of this planet.

Pythagoras and Sound

Many are aware that Pythagoras, the Greek mathematician from the sixth century B.C., is acknowledged as the father of geometry. However, few know that he had a school that taught not only the mystery of numbers, but also the use of sound to affect and heal the body, mind, and spirit. The first level of initiates learned the secrets of acoustical proportions. Pythagoras believed that the "Music of the Spheres," the sounds of the heavenly bodies as they moved through space, could be realized and was reflected in the sounds of vibrating strings. The second level of students learned further secrets of mathematics and numbers while they went through a stage of purification to receive this information. The third level of initiates was given direct knowledge of the transmuting and healing energies of sound and music.

Throughout history, we have had great philosophers and scientists who have acknowledged the power of sound to heal and transform. Music was not an art form, but a way of using energy and power to be respected and studied as a sacred science. The principles of vibration, which are at the core of these ancient beliefs, are still as relevant and true today as they were thousands of years ago. Unfortunately, today, much of this ancient knowledge has been forgotten.

Gratefully, we are on the cutting edge of a reemergence of the understanding about sound as a vehicle for self-transformation and healing. In April 2003, Jonathan presented at the "Science and Consciousness" conference; also presenting was Dr. Michio Kaku, one of the world's preeminent physicists, whose talk was on the unified field theory. He began explaining that Einstein and other great scientists weren't entirely correct. It wasn't simply $E=mc^2$. It was something greater than that. "Everything is music!" he declared. This statement came from a man whose widely hailed interpretation of the superstring theory postulates that there are many parallel dimensions that are inter-related through harmonically related vibrations. Dr. Kaku's statement that "Everything is music!" echoed what Jonathan had declared in his workshop. As the ancient Hindus have told us, *Nada Brahma*—the world is sound!

Sound as a Wave

Sound travels as a waveform, which, just like a wave in the ocean, goes up and down. These waves of sound are measured in cycles per second (called Hertz and abbreviated as Hz). This measurement is called the frequency of a sound. Slow-moving waves make bass sounds. Fast-moving waves make treble sounds. The lowest note on a piano makes a deep bass sound and has a frequency of 27.5 Hz. The highest note on a piano makes a treble sound and has a frequency of 4,186 Hz. We hear from around 16 Hz to around 16,000 Hz. Younger people whose hearing has not deteriorated due to auditory damage or age can hear up to 18,000 Hz or higher.

Just because we can't hear a sound doesn't mean it is not there.

Figure 1 Sound is a wave.

Dolphins can project and receive frequencies upwards of 180,000 cycles per second. That's more than ten times beyond our limit of hearing sound. Thus we'd like you to contemplate the idea that stems from the phrase "In the Beginning"—that everything and anything is sound. From the electrons moving around the nucleus of an atom to planets in distant galaxies moving around stars, everything is in motion. And if something is in motion, it is (conceptually, at least) putting out a vibration that may be perceived as sound, whether audible or not.

Resonance

Everything that vibrates has its own resonant frequency—that is, the frequency or vibration that is most natural and harmonious to it. We've all seen examples of resonance. When singers are able to shatter glass by making a sound, they've matched the resonance of the glass.

An experiment that is frequently used to demonstrate resonance in science classes is to hit a tuning fork and watch as the sound wave travels to another tuning fork of the same frequency, setting it in motion. This is often done by mounting the tuning forks on wooden boxes to help us hear the sound. If you listen closely, you can hear the tuning fork that has not been struck putting out a sound as a result of resonance with the struck one.

Everything in the universe vibrates and everything also has its own resonant frequency. This includes the chair you may be sitting on, the pages of this book, and, of course, your own body. Every organ, bone, tissue, and every part of your body is in a state of vibration and has its own resonance. Every part of your body is putting

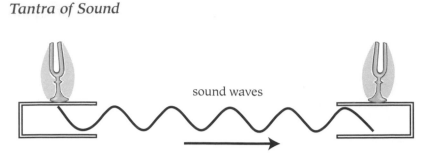

sound waves

Figure 2 Waves of one tuning fork setting the other tuning fork into resonance.

out a sound that is contributing to creating an overall harmonic of health. Our body is like a wonderful orchestra with each section playing the proper notes for what could be called the "Suite of the Self." This is analogous to a condition of health. In fact, when we are in a state of good health, we call this "sound" health.

However, what happens when the second-violin player loses his sheet music? He begins to play out of key, out of tune, out of rhythm and harmony with the rest of the orchestra. This is analogous to the condition of disease.

The basic principle of sound healing as well as any vibrational medicine is this: to restore the correct vibratory resonance to that part of the body that is vibrating out of harmony. To continue with our metaphor, it is giving back the correct sheet music to the second-violin player who has lost his music, so he can again play in tune with the orchestra, that is, our human body.

This basic principle of sound healing can be applied in numerous ways to situations in our lives, whether the situation is that a portion of our body is vibrating out of harmony and manifesting disease, or a portion of our psyche is out of tune with ourselves or others and is manifesting dysfunctional relationships. Just as we can use sound to restore the sheet music to that violin player, we can use sound to heal all aspects of being.

Through the use of sound healing techniques it is possible to examine many aspects of our existence, and come to new understandings about the way we live. We can enhance our daily lives. The simple laws of physics such as resonance that dictate how sound waves operate can also mirror aspects of our lives. Ancient mystics who created the Hermetic philosophy encoded these principles of sound and vibration with statements like, "As above, so below," realizing that the vibrations of a simple string mirrored many universal principles.

The waveform phenomenon of sound can be observed throughout life—everything is cyclical and has pulsations just like sound. Our seasons, our days, even our breath, demonstrate periodicity—the cyclical nature of waves. The next time you're caught in a huge traffic jam, realize that you're at the peak of a traffic waveform, and when it seems like there's no one else on the road, you're at the opposite end of this wave. Waves go up and down, just like the ocean.

Awareness of the waveform phenomena of life can be helpful, particularly if you are undergoing a calamitous episode in your life. If we remember that what we're going through is part of a wave, temporary and not permanent, this knowledge can help in stressful times.

Cymatics

This word "Cymatics" means waveform phenomena. It is from the Greek word *kyma,* which means waves, and was used to describe the experiments of a twentieth-century Swiss medical doctor named Hans Jenny. Dr. Jenny took many different materials (pastes, plastics, liquids), put them on a steel plate, and then vibrated the plate with sound. He found that these lifeless blobs of plastics or mounds of pastes would take on the most harmonious and lifelike forms when vibrated by sound. Among the hundreds of photographs taken by Dr. Jenny are pictures that look organic, some like human organs and others like microscopic life; in reality, they are of inorganic materials that looked like lifeless shapes moments before they were exposed to sound.

The photographs of his experiments are breathtaking in their

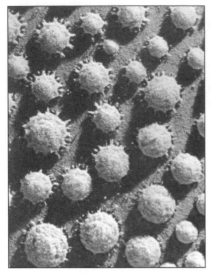

Figure 3 Cymatics picture of powder being vibrated and shaped by sound. Image taken from *Cymatics: A Study of Wave Phenomenon and Vibration* (combined vols. I and II) by Dr. Hans Jenny. © 2001 MACROmedia Publishing. Used by permission.

beauty and in the exquisite truth they expound—that sound creates form. While these forms may not be "alive," they certainly look life-like, appearing similar to cells in division or underwater sea life. These Cymatics experiments clearly echo the principle of "In the Beginning" that we have been discussing—sound as the fundamental creative source.

Figure 3 shows one of Dr. Jenny's Cymatics photographs. Before the sound resonated the plate, the powder was scattered haphazardly around; once the sound began to vibrate the plate, the powder organized itself into the most extraordinary of shapes.

Entrainment

Another vitally important aspect of sound is called entrainment. Christian Huygens, a Dutch scientist, discovered this in the seventeenth century. He had a room full of grandfather clocks with pendulums. These pendulum clocks were different sizes and shapes. One day, he set them all in motion at different times and then left the room. When he returned the next day, he found that all the clocks were locked in step—entrained—with the movements of the largest of these pendulum clocks.

Just as the pendulums of the clocks changed their rhythms to match the largest clock, so we are constantly being affected and changing our rhythms through encountering vibrations. Our bodies have many rhythms. Our heart rate, pulse rate, and breathing rate are all examples of this. In fact, our brains have pulsations and rhythms that are measured in cycles per second, just like sound frequencies.

Brain Waves

Our brain waves pulsate and oscillate at particular frequencies that can be measured like sound waves in cycles per second or Hertz (Hz). There are four basic delineations of different brain wave states based on the cycles per second of the brain.

• **Beta waves,** 14 to 20 Hz, are found in our normal waking state of consciousness. Beta waves are present when our focus of attention is on activities of the external world.

• **Alpha waves,** 8 to 13 Hz, occur when we daydream and are often associated with a state of meditation. Alpha waves become stronger and more regular when our eyes are closed.

• **Theta waves,** 4 to 7 Hz, are found in states of high creativity and have been equated with states of consciousness found in much shamanic work. Theta waves also occur in states of deep meditation and sleep.

• **Delta waves,** 0.5 to 3 Hz, occur in states of deep sleep or unconsciousness. Some of the newer brain wave work indicates that a state of deep meditation produces delta waves in conscious individuals.

Not only are there observable and verifiable rhythms in our body, but these rhythms can be influenced by sound. The fact that our brain waves, as well as our nervous systems, can be affected by sound will be of major significance as we begin to understand and explore the connection between sound, tantra, and our relationship to ourselves and each other.

One of us (Jonathan) named this phenomenon of sound being able to create entrainment "sonic entrainment." His groundbreaking research paper on this subject was first presented at the International Society for Music Medicine in 1989. The term "sonic entrainment" is now frequently used in psychoacoustics, the study of how sound affects our nervous system; we discuss sonic entrainment later in this book. For the moment, simply contemplate the fact that sound can change our nervous systems and brain waves. The implications are astounding.

Sound as Energy

We live in a world saturated with sound. From stereos to street noises, talking on telephones to the hum of refrigerators, sound is all around us and is affecting us. Most of us regard sound as simply something that goes into our ears and somehow gets transformed into a signal that ends up in our brain, allowing us to hear. This is certainly true—sound waves travel our auditory pathways, producing signals that ultimately make it to the part of our brain that processes these signals. We do indeed hear sound. What few people realize is that the aural experience not only allows us to hear, it also affects nearly all the cranial nerves, in particular, the tenth cranial nerve. This nerve affects the larynx, the bronchi, the heart, and the gastrointestinal tract. Thus sounds affect our voice, breathing, heart rate, and digestion.

In addition, few realize that sound is an energy that affects more than our ears and our ability to hear. "Ultrasonic beams can make, break or rearrange molecules and levitate objects in midair." Please read that last sentence again—it did not come from the *National Inquirer* but from the February 8, 1988, Science section of the prestigious newspaper the *New York Times*. Sound has the ability to rearrange molecular structure.

We are talking about an enormously powerful and profound energy that can do extraordinary things. Imagine the ability to rearrange molecules, and then envisage the implications. Realize what enhancing our personal lives through reducing stress, instilling calmness, and heightening consciousness through the focused use of sound can do. Begin to contemplate what it would mean if we learned to use sound to rearrange molecular structure.

The ability of sound to influence and affect each of us is of paramount importance as we continue on our journey. In order to understand more of how sound and tantra work together, let us examine in the next chapter the vibrational nature of the body.

~ 3 ~

The Body Vibrational

If we ask where the body ends, some would probably answer, our skin. No doubt ten or 20 years ago this would have been a typical response. But nowadays, with the awareness of ancient systems of healing and meditation, many understand that the physical body is just one of numerous energetic systems that exist and interrelate with each other. There are other vibrating fields, often called the subtle bodies, layered over the physical body. These subtle bodies have energy fields that vibrate at different rates. It is through our sound practices that we'll be resonating and shifting these energies. This is a major key in working with the tantra of sound.

Knowledge of these subtle bodies first manifested thousands of years ago in the ancient mystery schools of India, Egypt, China, and Tibet. The understanding of our bodies as being composed of different, interfacing energetic fields is one of the core concepts of the esoteric traditions found throughout the world. These energy bodies make up what is called the "aura," a word meaning atmosphere or light. It is a word usually defined as a multidimensional energy field made up of the emanations of each of the subtle bodies.

Different esoteric traditions have special names for the subtle energy bodies as well as their particular attributes and descriptions. While there are differences in the specifics of each of these subtle bodies, most sources are in agreement that these bodies become denser and more solidified until they end with the physical body. The most common descriptions of these bodies are as follows:

1. **Physical body:** As suggested, it ends at the skin.

2. **Etheric body:** This layer extends outward from the physical body for several inches and appears to provide a matrix of form for the physical body. This seems to be the energy field that many healers utilize. It is regarded as the repository of the universal life force (called chi, ki, prana, orgone, vayu, ruach, and other terms in various traditions). A wound on the physical body will appear as a disruption in the etheric body. Frequently, treating this disruption will help heal the physical body. Clairvoyants often describe the etheric body as being a grayish-white color, consisting of a matrix or a network of lines representing energy.

3. **Emotional body:** This body houses our feelings and emotions, likes and dislikes, sensual enjoyment and aesthetic appreciation. It can extend outward between six inches and a foot or more from the physical body. This subtle layer is the place where emotionally created thought forms such as fear seem to exist. Clairvoyants are able to sense past traumas here. Frequently, trapped emotional trauma will lead to imbalances in the physical body, and healers who work here are able to release these blockages and restore balance to the physical and emotional bodies. The emotional body is seen as full of ever-changing colors, which often represent the predominant emotional characteristics of a person at any given point in time. An angry person, for example, might have a predominance of red.

4. **Mental body:** This body houses the principles of the mind

and our thoughts. It is an energy field that begins approximately one foot from the physical body and extends an additional foot from there. It reflects the activity of the conscious and subconscious mind. This is where mental constructs and our belief systems exist. Thought forms derived from our intellect—our mind and mental processes—get lodged here, particularly belief systems that may not be of benefit to our lives and health. Healers will often work on the mental body, sometimes dissolving the thought forms that manifest these imbalanced energies on the physical body. By dissolving these thought forms from the mental body, such energy work will then heal the physical problem. The mental body is frequently seen as yellow.

5. **Astral body:** This body contains a blending of emotional and mental images, with some spiritual attributes as well. It is an energy field found approximately three feet from the physical body and extends from there for another foot. It is often perceived as the body that people utilize for out-of-body experiences (OBEs), also known as astral traveling. Thus it seems to be able to separate from the physical body and travel to higher realms of consciousness. Some suggest that it does not contain the complete essence of our being and thus is limited to the levels of consciousness to which it can travel. As with all the subtle bodies, the farther from the physical body, the less dense, more subtle, and more refined the vibration. Thus the frequency of the astral body is more refined than the previous bodies listed. Note: Some sources place this body between the etheric body and the emotional body.

6. **Causal body:** This body houses our memories from this and other lives. This energy body is found about four feet from the physical body and extends an additional foot from there. It is in this layer of subtle energy where many psychics can read past-life experiences from the Akashic records. Such experiences can affect actions and experiences in our present lifetimes. The causal body operates at a transcendent level of being and is extremely fine in its vibratory essence.

7. **Spiritual body:** This body encompasses all of our spiritual being. It is the least dense and most subtle of all these energetic bodies. It serves as the body of the higher self, or the totality of our essence. This energy body may extend several feet from the causal body—some suggest even farther. Thus our subtle bodies, particularly the higher vibratory bodies, are constantly interfacing and interacting with others' subtle bodies. These multidimensional, psychospiritual energy fields create waveforms of consciousness that are a part of the tantra, the web of existence that unites and unifies us all.

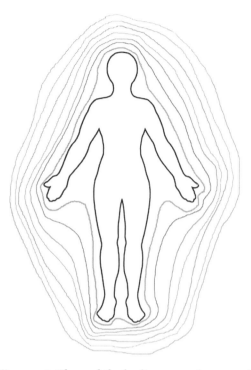

Figure 4 The subtle bodies extend outward from the physical body.

The names, as well as the order, of these subtle bodies may vary, depending on the metaphysical tradition describing them. The awareness of these subtle bodies, as previously stated, has existed for thousands of years and is found in esoteric traditions around the globe. Shamans and spiritual teachers alike have taught and utilized these bodies for healing and the evolution of consciousness. They are the basis of many healing methods including Ayurveda, Tibetan medicine, and acupuncture.

In terms of Western science and medicine, the subtle body energy system has yet to be sufficiently verified. This does not mean the subtle bodies do not exist but rather that the scientific instrumentation to measure and record them properly has not yet been invented, at least to the satisfaction of most of the scientific community. Little more than one hundred years ago, neither X-rays nor atomic particles were established scientific fact. Nor, for that matter, was the existence of the gorilla. Today, knowledge of the existence of X-rays and atomic particles, as well as their use in scientific and medical work, is commonplace. Gorillas have also been proven to be real.

No doubt when the scientific technology has developed to the point where the vibratory nature of the human being can be measured, knowledge of energy systems will become quite commonplace. In the 1940s, Semyon and Valentina Kirlian began experimenting in Russia with photographic plates exposed to high-frequency electrical fields. They observed that when a subject placed his finger or hand on the plate, some unknown substance appeared surrounding the physical part, often varying in brightness, depth, and size. They also observed correlations between the health and vitality of the subject and this unknown substance. The Kirlians believed that they had found verification of the aura, long claimed to be visible to psychics.

Much experimentation since that time has been conducted with Kirlian photography, as well as with other instrumentation to detect and corroborate the existence of the subtle bodies. Work to measure these subtle energies scientifically is even now being conducted in many laboratories throughout the world. Organizations such as the International Society for the Study of Subtle Energy and Subtle Energy Medicine meet each year and share cutting-edge knowledge of the body vibrational. New instrumentation is being developed that will one day record the different vibrations of the subtle bodies in a manner acceptable to Western scientists. We applaud the progress that is slowly occurring in this area and look forward to the day when doctors will not only look at X-rays and MRIs (magnetic resonance imaging scans), but subtle body scans as well.

Perhaps one of the reasons for the difficulty of scientifically proving the existence of these bodies is the fact that the vibrations that compose the different energy bodies are said to come from a divine source. This energy transduces (or changes frequency) through each energy level, becoming less subtle, slower in frequency, and denser in vibration until, at last, it becomes our physical body. We seem to be fairly adept at measuring those things that manifest as physical, but measuring the subtle energies has proven to be much more difficult for us.

An interesting analogy can be found with sound. As stated in the previous chapter, our ears can only hear sounds that travel between 16 Hz (very slow and deep) to 16,000 Hz (very fast and high). Therefore, for most of us, any sounds above this level are undetectable to us as sound. Those of you who have dogs and have blown dog whistles know that our limitations with regard to hearing sounds do not stop animals with greater hearing from perceiving them, nor do they negate the reality that these higher pitched sounds exist. Thus our limitations of hearing may be likened to our inability to detect frequencies of energy that create the energy and fields of energy around the body. Whether or not we can detect this energy, it still exists.

Of course, not everyone hears exactly the same. Some people can hear above 16,000 Hz, and some people can see beyond our normal range of vision, being able to actually see the subtle body energy and the auric fields. Many people can learn to sense the denser levels of the aura. Since Jonathan comes from a family of medical doctors (grandfather, father, and brother are all physicians), he fought furiously to deny this when he was first introduced to the idea of subtle energy. This was nearly 30 years ago, but a nurse who was teaching a workshop on therapeutic touch was patient with him. Finally, to Jonathan's amazement, he was able to detect energy outside the physical body. He learned how to assist in balancing this energy with his hands.

At the time, Jonathan was playing in a rock-and-roll band and he came back from this workshop in therapeutic touch a changed individual. He walked into band practice the next day and said hello to everyone. The bass player complained of being sick. Jonathan ran his hand in front of the bassist, keeping about two inches away from the physical body. It looked like he was just running his hands through the air. But then Jonathan said to the bass player, "Hmm . . . sore throat, huh?" The bassist's mouth dropped open in amazement, saying: "How did you know?" Jonathan then smoothed out the disruption and the bass player felt better.

Andi first became aware of feeling "energy" in 1972 when she was taking a class on healing at the Atlanta Institute of Metaphysics in Georgia. She was practicing some of the healing techniques being taught with a partner who had a bad headache. She began using her hands to soothe the etheric field around her partner's head, neck, and shoulder area. To her amazement, after about five minutes of concentrated focus, the person's headache began to dissipate. It was at that moment that she began to grasp the power inherent in the use of energy for healing.

In fact, our ability to transmit and receive energy is something we can all learn to work with naturally and effectively. Deep in some subconscious part of ourselves, we know that we can assist with this energy even by simply putting our hand on a place that has pain. Frequently, if we have enough training, we can relieve the pain. It's actually very simple.

Experiment

Here is an exercise that will begin to help you develop your ability to feel subtle energy.

Rub your hands briskly together for a few seconds. Then slowly pull your hands apart and begin moving them near each other in circular patterns. You'll probably sense a tingling sensation in your hands.

Move your hands close to each other and then farther away. See how far you can move your hands apart before you stop feeling the tingling sensation.

If you're with a partner, do this with them. Rub your hands together and then hold them a few inches in front of the other person's hands. See if you can feel their energy.

Have one of the partners close their eyes while the other moves their hands in front and then away, while the one with closed eyes tries to tell if they can feel the energy.

This is an excellent technique for learning to feel the auric field of another. You'll be amazed at how frequently accurate you both will be, even at the beginning. This, incidentally, is your first tantric exercise because as soon as you start dealing with sensing and working with energy, you're dealing with tantra.

What is most important with regard to our understanding about the body vibrational is that it involves a feedback system. If you can influence the energy body, you can influence the physical body, and if you can influence the physical body, you affect the energy body. This is how energy medicine works. It's why Jonathan was able to feel the sore throat of his bass player at band practice those many years ago. And why Andi was able to effect the dissipation of the headache of the person in her healing class. What Jonathan felt as he moved his hand through the other person's energy field was a disruption in the throat area. Something did not feel smooth and was vibrating out of ease—it felt different. That was how Jonathan knew it was a sore throat.

Frequently, one can work solely on the energy bodies and bring about rapid and amazing healings on the physical body. This is the basis of much energy medicine, including sound therapy. As we will soon discover, using sound with the physical and subtle bodies can enhance healing and balance and increase intimacy with ourselves and our partner. It can assist us in feeling the connectedness with the web of life.

The Chakras

We have described the different subtle bodies and stated that these different bodies all vibrate at different frequencies, becoming denser and slower the closer we actually get to the physical body.

These bodies all represent different energies; what they have in common is the chakra system.

The word *chakra* is Sanskrit and means "wheel." Chakras are sensed and seen as spinning discs or wheels of energy. There are seven main chakras located vertically along the center of the body. Chakras are vortices of vibration, places where the energy from subtle bodies becomes denser and denser until this energy manifests in the physical body. As the chakras become more dense, they first become the acupuncture meridians and points before manifesting in the physical body. In the Hindu tradition, the *nadis,* or "sub chakras" as they're sometimes called, are seemingly identical with the acupuncture points.

Chakras can be seen as light, felt as vibration, and heard as sound, and, as we have mentioned, they are perceived through touch. So after you have learned to sense subtle energy with your hands, if you then move your hand from below the trunk to above the head, you will begin to feel seven pulsating areas of energy. These are the chakras.

As stated, the seven main chakras are located centrally along the front and back of the body. They are focal points of manifestation for the energy that makes up the subtle body. Here are their locations (as well as their Sanskrit names and their attributes):

1. The **base chakra** *(Muladhara)* is located in the pelvic cavity, between the genitals and the anus. It is associated with the element of earth. The adrenal glands, activated during fight-or-flight conditions, are frequently linked to this chakra. It is related to the energy of grounding and survival. This chakra is most often described as deep red in color.

2. The **sacral chakra** *(Svadhisthana)* is located about three inches below the navel. This chakra is associated with the sexual organs, gonads, and the element of water. It is related to the life energy of reproduction and the energy of creativity. This chakra is frequently described as orange in color.

3. The **navel chakra** *(Manipura)* is located around the navel. This

chakra is associated with the digestive organs, pancreas, stomach, gallbladder, and the element of fire. Power, self-mastery, self-esteem, and intuition are attributes of this chakra. The color yellow is often associated with this chakra.

4. The **heart chakra** *(Anahata)* is located in the center of the chest. It is associated with the heart, blood, respiratory and circulatory systems, and also with the element of wind. This is the chakra of love and compassion and is said to be the chakra from which all healing originates. It is most frequently visualized with the color green.

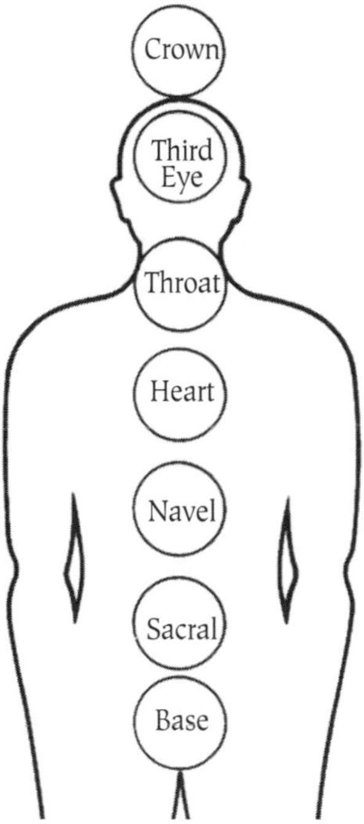

5. The **throat chakra** *(Vishudda)* is located at the throat. It is associated with organs of speech and hearing, our vocal apparatus and our ears, as well as with the thyroid gland. It is related to

Figure 5 The seven chakras and their approximate positions.

the element of ether, or space. This is the chakra of communication and self-expression. The predominant color seen for this chakra is light blue.

6. The **brow chakra** *(Ajna)* is located about half an inch above and between the eyebrows. Popularly known as the "third eye," this chakra is associated with the brain, and often with the master gland of the endocrine system, the pituitary gland. It is primarily related with the attributes of imagination, psychic ability, and the seeking of God. It is the "inner eye" of wisdom and is frequently seen as indigo in color. It is said that once this chakra is awakened, one meets one's Divine Self.

7. The **crown chakra** *(Sahasrara)* is located at the top of the head. It is said to control every aspect of the body and mind and is associated with full enlightenment and union with God. This chakra is

rarely fully opened, except in cases of very high spiritual beings. The halo that surrounds the heads of saintly beings in spiritual paintings is the representation of an activated crown chakra. This chakra is frequently seen as violet, as well as golden light.

The most important things about the chakras are:

1. They can be perceived through touch, sight, or sound.

2. They are influenced and affected by our sense of touch, sight, and particularly sound.

3. They are the basis of much tantric practice, affecting our relationship to self and others.

As mentioned earlier, the chakras are the interface between the subtle bodies. As the bodies become denser until they manifest in the physical, so then does the energy of the chakras. As we learn to work with the chakras, we'll also learn to work with the energy of the different bodies. Thus it is through working with our chakras that we can begin to experience balance within us. Through experiencing this balance we also become aware of the web of tantra—the interconnectedness of all things. This balance and alignment will assist in creating personal health and wellness. In addition, it is through resonating and sounding the chakras that much of the deep intimacy and energy work that we do will occur. Sound can assist us in generating inner balance and harmony and help us harmonize with others as well.

In the beginning of this chapter we posed the question, "Where does the body end?" In truth, the body vibrational, composed of various subtle energy bodies including the chakras, may extend many feet away from the physical body. Thus two people standing some distance from each other can still interface with each other due to their energy fields.

Through understanding how to affect our chakras and our subtle bodies using sound, it is possible for us to learn to affect and interface with the energy of someone else. This is one of the principles of using sound as tantra. An extremely important aspect of understanding this phenomenon has to do with *intent*, explained in the next chapter.

$\backsim$ 4 $\eqsim$

The Power of Intent

Back in the late 1980s, Jonathan had just completed a master's degree in independent study from Lesley University, which involved researching the uses of sound and music for healing. After his master's thesis was complete, he began turning this material into a book. He continued amassing information on the relationship between sound and healing and, in particular, between sound and the chakras. He found dozens of systems that used sound to resonate the chakras.

The trouble was that all these systems were very different from one another, and none of them seemed to be in agreement. One system would use a particular mantra to resonate a chakra, and another system would use the same mantra to resonate a different chakra. Or he'd find different mantras from different teachers that resonated the same chakra. There was a wide variety of systems of sound that resonated the chakras according to the spiritual master, the culture, or the tradition involved. Jonathan found this confusing.

"I knew there had to be a connecting link between these systems—some understanding that explained this conundrum, how different teachers and masters could have success with such a variety of sounds," he said. However, it didn't make any sense to him. He remembers sitting at his computer with his head in his hands in a state of intellectual angst. How could there be so many conflicting systems of chakra resonance and sound healing in general that all seemed to work?

Suddenly, he heard a voice say: "It is not only the frequency of the sound that creates the effect of the sound. It is also the *intention* of the person creating the sound that equally affects the sound."

He typed out the words *"Frequency + Intent = Healing"* and as they appeared on the computer screen, he knew he had found the explanation for the extraordinary variety and difference in sounds used effectively by people for resonance and healing. To this day, this formula continues to work effectively as an explanation, giving valuable understanding to the many healers working with sound.

Frequency

Frequency is one form of measurement for sound. It measures sound through its rate of vibrations (or cycles per second). There are other ways to measure sound besides frequency. We use the word frequency in Jonathan's formula "Frequency + Intent = Healing" to understand the physical sound itself. In another related formula, "Vocalization + Visualization = Manifestation," we substitute the word "Vocalization" for "Frequency," and in this formula it refers to physical sound that is vocalized.

In the formula, "Frequency + Intent = Healing," healing refers to the effect or outcome of using the sound. Since this equation was initially included in Jonathan's book *Healing Sounds,* it was obviously the desired outcome for the use of the sound. However, as the other formula, "Vocalization + Visualization = Manifestation" demonstrates, this outcome clearly can be whatever one wants to have manifested through making the sound.

Intent

Intent is the energy behind the sound. It is the consciousness we have when making and projecting a sound. It is our thoughts, visualizations, feelings—the energy of our consciousness that travels on the sound and is perceived energetically by the person receiving (hearing) the sound. Many years ago, Steven Halpern, a healing music pioneer, wrote: "Sound is a carrier wave of consciousness." This is another way of describing the relationship of sound and consciousness and a basis for using intention.

To the ancients, sound was not only an energy form or a power, it was in many respects a direct representation of the Divine. As such, sound was given the respect and reverence of divine forces. Sadly, this understanding of the power of sound has been lost until recently, and with it, the power of intent.

By projecting intention into the sound, different experiences and effects can be created. Thus two people can potentially create the same sound with different intentions, and manifest two different effects. One could make a sound and project healing energy into it, while another could make the same sound with the opposite effect, depending on the intention. From our perspective, intent may be the most important and powerful part of the formula.

If frequency (or vocalization) is the physical counterpart of sound, then intent (or visualization) is the spiritual counterpart of the sound, and together they create the outcome of the sound (the healing or the manifestation).

Frequency of course is easy to demonstrate. In fact, almost any physical aspect of sound (such as its sound energy or decibel level, which is how loud or soft a sound is) can be effectively measured with scientific instruments. Intent, however, is a bit more difficult to measure. This is, if you like, akin to the difficulties we currently have measuring the chakras and the subtle body. However, with the use of kinesiology we can begin to measure intention.

Kinesiology

Kinesiology is a method of muscle testing that allows a practitioner to determine the strengths and weaknesses of organs, bones, acupuncture meridians, even the chakras, in relationship to different substances such as foods or drugs. It can even be used to check whether a sound is beneficial for us. The practice of kinesiology is now flourishing in many holistic health communities, utilized by a range of practitioners from chiropractors to medical doctors. In fact, several well-known medical doctors, including Dr. John Diamond and Dr. David Hawkins, have written on the subject.

With kinesiology, when your body encounters a substance that may not be good for it (for instance, sugar), your muscles are weakened. When your body encounters a substance that is good for it (for instance, a piece of organically grown fruit), your muscles become strong. While any muscle can be used, many kinesiological practitioners use the deltoid muscle of the arm for testing. If you held some sugar in your hand and extended your arm out horizontally, your deltoid muscle would become weakened if sugar is not good for you, and it would then be easy for someone to push down your arm. However, if you held an organically raised orange in your hand, this muscle would be strengthened if the fruit is good for you and it would be more difficult for someone to push down your arm.

The simplest explanation for this is that substances such as the organic orange have positive, life-affirming energy that strengthens our muscles, physical body, and subtle bodies. Substances that are not good for us lack life energy and short-circuit the systems of the body vibrational by weakening us; conversely, substances that are good for us amplify the energy of the body vibrational. Not only physical substances, but various vibratory forms, such as sound, can also be tested for positive, life-affirming qualities. The following story demonstrates the use of kinesiology with regard to this.

An Experiment Using Kinesiology

Years ago, an experiment was done with a group of people. They sat in a circle by the ocean with a cassette recorder in the middle of the group. The people meditated blissfully (and silently), projecting love onto the sound of the ocean that was then being recorded. Next, a new cassette was put in, the record button pressed and this time they generated anger. Not a word was said as the sound of the ocean was recorded. Finally, the group of people left the area and just the sound of the ocean, without anyone around, was recorded onto a third cassette.

Then the real work began. A skilled practitioner of kinesiology muscle-tested people as they listened to the sounds of the ocean on each of the three cassettes. Three separate tests were conducted for each of the three tapes, which all sounded the same. No one knew which tape they were listening to, not even the kinesiological tester. It was just the sound of the ocean. But the results were radically different.

First, the recording of the ocean without anyone around made people strong. As you might expect, the sounds of nature are nurturing to our body, mind, and spirit, and indeed this was true with the kinesiological testing that day.

Second, the recording of the ocean with people blissfully projecting love made people test even stronger. It was remarkable how powerful this sound was for the people being tested. They became rock solid while this ocean sound played.

Finally, the recording of the "angry ocean," the one into which people projected anger, produced different kinesiological results, although it sounded like the other ocean recordings. People tested weak. The difference, of course, was the intention of the people infusing the sound.

Thus you can take the same sound, project two different intentions on that sound, and the outcome of that sound will be different. Or you can take two different sounds, put the same intention on those sounds, and the outcome can be the same. This explains how there can be so many people working with sounds that are very different and yet having similar results—their intentions are the same. Thus, Frequency + Intent = Healing.

We find that this principle using frequency and intent is especially true for people self-creating vocalized sound. Depending on the visualization used, a person is often able to manifest her desired intention using vocalized sound. This phenomenon of verifying visualization is, of course, more difficult to validate—even using kinesiology. For this, we must depend on the subjective accounts of people who report to us what they have experienced. However, if one person knows how to project energy onto a sound, and another person knows how to consciously perceive this energy, they could report what they experience, and verify the equation Vocalization + Visualization = Manifestation.

For example, one person, might make the sound *OH* at the frequency of 256 Hz (a C note) while visualizing peace and the color purple, and the person receiving this sound feels peace and purple. Another person might make the sound *EEE* at the frequency of 384 Hz (a G note) and project the same visualization of purple and peace; it can still be received even though it is a completely different sound. Or two people might make the same vowel sound at the same frequency, but project two different energies onto the sound. The person receiving the sound can perceive these different energies. This has been our experience year after year, working with many psychics and spiritually attuned people.

Feeling

Recently, the importance of the feeling that is projected onto sound has come to our attention. This is another aspect of intentionalized sound, and rather than the intention coming purely from our mind as a thought or visualization, it is coming from our heart through our feeling. Much of this awareness has come primarily from the exceptional work of spiritual scientist Gregg Braden.

In his groundbreaking book *The Isaiah Effect*, he says the most powerful form of prayer involves not asking for something but being in a state of appreciation as though it has already occurred. Thus, rather than "Please help me," the words "Thank you for your help!" seem to be more effective.

Using prayer to ask for something, as in the first example, is coming from a consciousness of the lack of it, and therefore coming from a fear-based consciousness. The second phrase, which involves "Thank you," comes from a state of appreciation, as though that which you are asking for has already occurred; therefore this comes from a love-based consciousness. This feeling of appreciation is similar to being in a heartfelt state comparable to love.

Researchers at the Institute of HeartMath, based in California, have shown that this state of appreciation creates a coherent electromagnetic resonance between the brain and heart. The electromagnetic field generated by the heart is 60 times greater than the electromagnetic field of the brain. This means that prayers coming from the heart produce a greater electromagnetic field response. Thus prayer created through appreciation seems to be more powerful, as is prayer that is sounded aloud.

There is something about the vocalization or sounding of a prayer that gives it more energy and life than when it is silently recited. Perhaps it's because, as the ancient mystics told us (and now our modern scientists have validated), everything is in a state of vibration. The fact that audible sound through song and chant has been the major form of prayer in practically every tradition is certainly a validation that people around the globe have intuitively known for a long time that sound is a key to enhancing prayer.

While this book is not specifically about prayer, both of us are advocates of the power of love and compassion as part of the tantric experience. We both use sound to project energy, not only to ourselves and each other, but also to the planet. We primarily project this energy of love and compassion from the heart. Certainly, in the work that we do with sound, we utilize all the chakras to resonate and project sound. No one chakra is better or more important than the others. They are all vital and necessary for our existence. As we note in workshops and other teaching occasions, projecting energy from all the chakras is ideal. We do, however, suggest that if there is one chakra where the energy could be most effectively amplified, empowered, and utilized, it is the heart. Kindness, appreciation, and compassion are vital ingredients in maintaining a loving connection with ourselves, others, and the web of life.

When two people are focusing their feelings of understanding and loving-kindness toward each other, sounds projected from the heart chakra are often found to be highly beneficial. Even the simple sound of *AH* with the intention of love being projected from the heart chakra can often bring about a state of inner peace, thus opening up the channels of love. When sounding with a partner, or by oneself, the vibration creates a change in the subtle bodies as well as the physical body.

Entrainment versus Entertainment

We are advocates of using sound as a healing and transformational tool and we believe that there are no "bad" or "wrong" self-created sounds, as long as they are projected with the energy of love. So many of us had an experience in our youth when someone (perhaps a well-meaning music teacher) told us to sing quietly or maybe just mouth the words. How many of us are still searching for the proverbial bucket that we can use to carry a tune in?

With regard to the tantra of sound, none of this matters. We are not talking about using sound as a tool for entertainment and going out to sing in a nightclub or some other venue. We are writing about the use of sound as a tool for entrainment—to shift and change vibrational rates. With regard to this, the energy that we project onto the sound—our intent—is a primary aspect on which to focus. To repeat, if we can always use the intention of love, our sounds will always be of benefit.

Jonathan remembers one of his last studio sessions in Boston when he was asked to record version after version of a simple guitar line. Jonathan normally preferred to go in and record a track on the first or second try because his energy was normally upbeat and inspirational. In this case, however, the producer prided himself on having "perfect ears" and he found something wrong with every take that occurred. Jonathan continued for what seemed like hours until he got the part perfect and it was acceptable for this producer.

When Jonathan listened closely, he could indeed hear the technical perfection of the guitar part. But he could also *feel* the anger and frustration that had gone into creating the part and realized that, on some subtle level, any listener would also feel this. One of the things he always does now is to make sure that the energy he is projecting onto any of his recordings is the best possible and always filled with the energy of love. And if he ever finds himself stressed out in the recording studio, he turns his equipment off and then returns only when he feels back in balance.

The importance of intent, visualization, and feelings cannot be understated with regard to the tantra of sound. The sound we create is obviously important, and we will indeed be sharing some powerful sounds with you in the upcoming chapters. However, the consciousness that we project onto the sound is equally important. This is something we must remember.

The Best Time to Focus Intent

A question often arises as to when is the best time to focus intent. We suggest and many others believe that it is the still point between the in-breath and out-breath. It is in this still point that a harmonious wave occurs between the heart and the brain.

Take a breath, and just at that point after you have breathed in, as you are momentarily holding your breath, focus a thought, an image, or a feeling (it is to be hoped, the feeling of love) down to your heart. Then, when you breathe out, you'll find that your breath has been encoded with your heart consciousness. It's that simple.

Please note, however, we believe the more comfortable and at ease you are in any activity or exercise suggested in this book, the more adept you will be at it. Thus while we may give you suggestions, such as projecting intent at a particular time in the breathing cycle, we by no means are rigid. We are fluid in our beliefs. If this or something else we may suggest does not feel in resonance with you or is uncomfortable, please feel free not to use it. Remember there is no "right" or "wrong" way of using sound to enhance your deeper connections of love.

Fluidity seems to be a key to maintaining health and balance, and is essential in terms of tantra. Being rigid constricts energy; being fluid allows energy to flow. Sound is fluid—it constantly changes. Thus the more flowing and graceful you become using sound, the more effective you will be with regard to the tantra of sound.

Part II

Basic Practices

≈ 5 ≈

Breath and Toning

Before we begin this chapter, pause for a moment and take a slow, deep breath. Hold your breath for a few seconds and then slowly release it. Perhaps you might do it again. As you do, observe yourself and notice any changes that may occur. By taking a few conscious deep breaths, you have made remarkable changes in your heartbeat and respiration, and even affected your brain waves.

The science of breath has been the subject of many great teachings. Books have been written on the subject. It is the basis of many esoteric studies, including that of yoga. There are indeed many different schools on the proper way of breathing. Some believe that proper breath occurs only through the nose. Others believe that through the mouth is the only way to breathe. Still others combine the two approaches.

Breath is the essence of life; it is sacred. Many spiritual traditions are aware of this, and their words for breath incorporate this awareness of the life energy in breath. This energy is called *prana* in the Hindu traditions. In the Orient, it is known as *chi* or *ki*. In the Hebrew tradition, one word for breath is *ruach*, which is also the same as the word for "spirit." Wilhelm Reich, Sigmund Freud's disciple, called this energy "orgone" and spent many years studying its power. This energy goes by many different names in the various cultures, countries, and spiritual paths on our planet. Yet it is the same. It is the energy of life—the energy of the breath.

As you breathe in, your body takes on a charge of this energy. As you hold your breath, your body builds this energy charge. As you release your breath, your body releases this charge. This is a simplification of the science of breath, called *pranayama* in the Hindu tradition. Yet in its simplicity there is much truth in these statements about breath, for when we focus our awareness on the power of breath, we can regulate and change our energetic bodies.

As briefly discussed in the previous chapter, fluidity is the basis of much higher spiritual understanding and knowledge. We therefore will not be rigid about any of our subjects, including breath. We believe that whatever works best for you and is comfortable for you should be the usual method of practice, whether it is breathing, making sound, or making love. We simply may have helpful suggestions.

Focusing your awareness on the power of breath is one of these suggestions—not as an overall activity (unless that is appropriate for you), but as an experience and an experiment in consciousness. To repeat: As you breathe in, your body takes on a charge of energy. As you hold your breath, your body builds this energy charge. As you release your breath, your body releases this charge of energy. It is amazing to breathe consciously in this manner, even if for a short while.

There are many variations on the theme of breathing techniques. Some people recommend taking an in-breath for four seconds, holding it for four seconds, and then releasing it for four seconds. Others recommend breathing in for eight seconds, holding for eight seconds, and releasing for eight seconds. Still others believe that breathing in for four seconds, holding for eight seconds, and releasing for four seconds is the best method. We suggest taking slow, deep breaths and experimenting with these suggestions. Remember, doing what feels comfortable and appropriate for you is our rule of thumb.

Diaphragmatic Breathing

With regard to taking deep breaths, we suggest that whether you breathe in through your nose or your mouth, that you get your breath as deep down into your lungs and belly as possible. This is called diaphragmatic breathing, which means to breathe down into your diaphragm, that part of your body just below your rib cage and lungs (see figure 6). If, as you breathe in, your rib cage and stomach begin to expand, then you are probably breathing in this manner. It allows for the greatest amount of air to enter your body.

Many of you may remember being shown how to breathe in school, with your shoulders raised and your stomach and rib cage firm and unmoving. This approach to breathing has also been taught in the military. It is useless in terms of expanding your air capacity. If you take a deep breath and find that your shoulders are rising, you are most likely not doing diaphragmatic breathing. You may also find yourself feeling tense. If this is the case, it might be useful to learn to breathe in a different manner. Here is a suggestion:

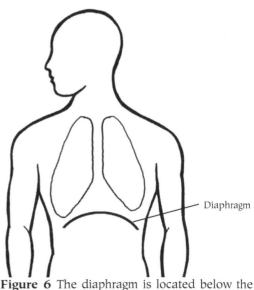

Figure 6 The diaphragm is located below the lungs.

Lying on the floor, put your hands on your stomach and take a deep breath. As you breathe in, focus your intention on bringing the air into the deepest part of your lungs and belly. Imagine your stomach as a balloon that you're blowing up. Watch as your belly rises with each breath as you breathe in. Then, breathe out and feel your stomach contract as the air is pushed out of your lungs. Do this again and again, until it begins to feel natural. Congratulations, you are now doing diaphragmatic breathing.

Diaphragmatic breathing, incidentally, is a natural way to breathe. If you watch infants, you'll see it's what they do. Sometimes we forget what is natural, so it's helpful to be reminded. So we remind you to breathe down into your stomach. If you're finding this difficult, remember that you once breathed like this, when you were a baby, and you can learn to do it again.

By breathing in this manner, you are increasing the supply of oxygen to your bloodstream, giving all the organs of your body more energy. Slow, deep, breathing not only oxygenates your body and brain, but it also slows down your heart rate and brain waves, helping induce calm and relaxation. This is excellent for your health as it reduces stress, which is a major cause of disease. If you're interested in learning more about breathing, we recommend *Conscious Breathing* (Bantam, 1995) by Gay Hendricks, Ph.D.

As you combine your focused awareness (intention) of the energy of your breath with slow, deep breathing, you assist your physical and subtle bodies by bringing still greater energy into your body. In the Far East, there are said to be "Breatharians," people whose study of pranayama has led them to be able to exist solely on the power of their breath. They do not eat, but get their nourishment from their breath. While Breatharians no doubt have practiced and developed certain breathing techniques that may be extraordinary, it seems to us that this is another example of the power of intent; even though these Breatharians may be able to supercharge their breath with energy, and not need food, they are still basically breathing into their lungs. There is no secondary organ that has been developed—at least in the physical body—that is used to process air differently. The conscious awareness and attention/intention of their breathing seem to be what enables them to use breath to sustain themselves.

Breath is the source of life, and it is also the source of sound. You cannot make sound, at least any vocally created sound, without breath. Thus before we begin to work with self-created sounds and tones, be sure you are able to breathe as fully and powerfully as possible.

Toning

The next exercises in this chapter focus on making self-created vocal sounds, or toning. This term was first used by Laurel Elizabeth Keyes in her book *Toning* (DeVorss, 1973). Toning most frequently describes the use of elongated vowel sounds to create resonance, harmony, and balance. It is the basis for producing vibrational shifts for health and transformation. A simple and natural concept, toning can be a powerful tool. In reality we tone all the time, whether it's a yawn when we're tired or a moan when we're in pain. Toning helps release trauma and blockages. Toning is an excellent tool for resonating our physical and subtle bodies.

We now invite you to experience the following basic toning technique, which can give you a feel for using your voice to make sounds:

Take a slow, deep breath and allow a simple *AH* sound to ride on your out-breath. (If you like, you can add an H and make it *HAH*—whatever works better for you.)

Let the gentle, relaxed sound emerge from you as you slowly breathe out. For the moment, don't attempt to sing this *AH*—simply let it be carried forth on your breath so that it's more of a sigh than anything else.

Breathe in again slowly and deeply, and then release the air while making the very soft and relaxed sound. What are you experiencing as this happens?

Try it again. Check yourself out. What's happening as you make the *AH* sound?

Make the gentle *AH* sound three times. Then be in silence for a moment. Observe your experience.

After making this *AH* sound, make it a few more times until you feel comfortable with the tone you are creating.

Then slowly begin to raise the volume of the *AH*, making it louder and more audible. Do this three times, and then be in silence, checking yourself out when you've stopped.

Sounding the *AH* can often bring about a state of inner peace, thus opening up the channels of love. It is a powerful sound, particularly useful for generating compassion, a key to the transformation of consciousness.

What Is the *AH* Sound?

The *AH* sound is a sacred seed syllable. This is a primordial sound of creation, and a sacred mantra in many Eastern traditions. It is also a vowel sound—a divinely inspired sound that is considered sacred in many traditions.

A gentle form of the *AH* sound is found in many of the names of gods and goddesses on the planet, such as Tara, Buddha, Krishna, Yahweh, Yeheshua, Saraswati, Wakantanka, and Quan Yin. It is also found in many sacred words, such as Amen, Alleluia, and Aum. As a seed syllable, the *AH* is universal and may be utilized differently in different traditions, depending on its purpose. According to many mystical traditions the world over, the *AH* sound is often the sound of the heart chakra. This chakra, located in the center of the chest, is the energy center associated with love, compassion, and feeling. Indeed, when many people think about the energy of love, they express it as an *AH* sound. Many spiritual masters believe that the activation of this chakra is most helpful for achieving higher consciousness and enlightenment. Most agree that the energy of love and the heart is the primary, essential energy of the universe.

Many people agree that the *AH* sound is the first sound that is created when we are born—the sound expressed on the exhalation of the first breath. The *AH* sound is often also the last sound we make, riding on the energy of our final exhalation. This use of the *AH* sound may be effective for those involved in hospice work.

In Tibetan Buddhism, there is a co-meditation technique that uses the *AH* sound. Chanting *AH* as a group (or even just breathing together) allows people to attune and resonate with one another. It seems that the heartbeat, respiration, and brain waves of two or more people entrain through breathing or sounding *AH* together.

We often recommend the *AH* as a sound for people who want to work with mantras in groups. The reason for this, as has been previously discussed, is that *AH* is a transformative sound, yet most people know of it only as a vowel sound, and thus it defies association with any spiritual denomination or description as a mantra. While other sounds such as *OM* might be rejected by certain audiences because they are recognized as Eastern mantras or coming from another spiritual tradition, the sounding of an *AH* is acceptable by everyone regardless of their background, culture, or religion. Thus it is possible to get people from around the world, regardless of belief systems, to sound an *AH*.

We have had exceptional results using the *AH* sound for "World Sound Healing Day," a global event that we coordinate each year using sound as a vehicle to manifest peace on our planet. People sound forth the *AH* while generating the energy of appreciation and compassion and sending it out to our planet. Participants have reported to us that they can feel waves of love rolling through the planet during the times of these group soundings, even though many of us are separated by hundreds, if not thousands of miles.

An Exercise for the *AH* Sound

Projecting the *AH* sound while feeling the energy of appreciation in the heart area seems to be an outstanding technique for using sound to generate compassion. We now invite you to explore and experiment with the *AH* sound using the following technique.

Begin by breathing slowly and deeply, using diaphragmatic breathing.

As you're breathing in this manner, think of something you feel appreciative of, something for which you are grateful. Think of something that has brought you joy and happiness. It could be a person or an animal, perhaps a child or a parent or a loved one, or a beloved pet. It could be a place you've been; perhaps an image of a beautiful sunrise or a wonderful moment at the beach or something similar. Use whatever image or thought helps inspire a feeling of appreciation in you.

As you are breathing and feeling this energy of appreciation, begin to sound *AH* so that it gently rides out on the breath. Make this sound three times while you are in this state of appreciation.

Now stop for a moment, and check yourself out. What do you observe? Do you feel any sensations—perhaps a subtle or gentle tingle in the center of your chest?

Take a couple more deep breaths and focus your attention so that as you breathe in, you visualize your breath coming into the center of your chest. As you breathe out, visualize it exiting through the center of your chest.

Now add a very gentle *AH* sound. As you are sounding, feel the *AH* sound projecting energy outward from the center of your chest.

Take three more breaths with the *AH* sound. Stop again and check yourself out. If it feels comfortable, increase the volume of the *AH*; if not, continue making the sound at the same volume.

As you make this *AH* sound again, think of a color that you'd like to encode on the sound. Project this onto the *AH* sound. Visualize any color that feels comfortable to you.

If you wish to extend making this *AH* sound, please do so. Continue feeling this state of appreciation. Feel yourself being at peace.

When you have finished this exercise, be in silence for a few moments to perceive any shifts and changes that may have occurred. Do you feel different now from when you began this exercise? Check yourself out. What do you observe?

There are several components to this exercise: (1) using a deep breathing technique; (2) feeling the energy of appreciation; (3) making a sound that is comfortable for you and experiencing that resonance in your body; and (4) adding color or other visualizations onto the sound.

This exercise, while simple, is beneficial and therapeutic. It can slow down your heart rate, respiration, and brain waves. It even creates coherence between your heart and your brain. It helps reduce stress and produces the beneficial results of relaxation, assisting and enhancing your well-being. If you are feeling out of harmony, making the *AH* sound in this manner is effective for helping create balance.

Keys to Assist You

One of the keys to being able to do the previous exercise is to practice. The more experience you have creating intentional sound, the easier it becomes. The more experience you have feeling the sound resonate in different parts of your body, the easier it will be to do this.

Another important key is that when working with your self-created sounds, one of the most important steps you can take to successfully produce a transformational and healing sound is to remember that there are no good or bad, right or wrong self-created sounds. When we engage in these practices, we are working with the principles of entrainment (not entertainment). There is no need for self-criticism; being nonjudgmental is a key to working successfully with sound.

Also, remember to be as relaxed as possible when you are making the *AH* sound. Project onto the sound as much love and appreciation as you can. Don't judge yourself about whether or not you performed well. Perhaps the greatest suggestion we can give to anyone working with sound is to become a "vehicle" for the sacred sound—"Lord, make me an instrument!" We like to tell people in our workshops that when creating sacred sound, you are a vessel, a conduit, because sacred sound is not coming from you but through you.

Silence after Sounding

The importance of silence cannot be overstated. Silence is the most important place to be because here the greatest shifts and changes occur from the sounds you have just made. Honor the silence in each exercise involving sound given in this book. Always be in silence after making the sounds. Many times when people first become aware of the power of sound, they become so infatuated by sound that they ignore the importance of sound's opposite polarity—silence. Please honor the power of silence after each sound experience you have.

Silence allows the sound to penetrate the physical body, making shifts and changes on molecular levels, affecting our cells, our DNA—everything that is physical. Silence also enables the frequency shifts in our subtle body, creating the space for the sound to permeate our chakras, aura, and all our subtle bodies.

Be Gentle with Yourself

Perhaps the only "do not" in this book is: *Do not strain your voice.* As always, comfort and fluidity are important. If you strain yourself, whether it's vocally or in any other fashion, you stop your fluidity and promote stress, and you also run the risk of damaging yourself physically. We do not subscribe to the "no pain/no gain" consciousness. We do subscribe to the importance of being gentle and loving with yourself—self-acceptance of the unique expression of life that you are.

Another observation about sound is that frequently when people first discover its power, they think that more is better. This is common in the West, related to many other things besides sound. Many believe that more sound is better, or that louder sound is better. Sometimes the most subtle sounds can create the greatest changes. We have observed extraordinary frequency shifts through the gentle use of sound and the power of love.

Once again, we ask that you begin gently, regardless of which exercise you or a partner are engaged in. As you raise your sound energy volume (the decibel levels, the loudness of the sound), do this slowly. As soon as you reach any point of minor discomfort, you are being too loud. Cut back on the volume. The same is true for the frequency or note you may be sounding. Don't strain. If it becomes difficult to sound a note that may be pitched too high for you, make it lower in a range that is comfortable for you. Or if the note's pitch is too low and it's difficult and uncomfortable for you to sound, then make it higher. Do whatever it takes to get you into your zone of comfort.

In the next chapter, we present a more comprehensive technique using sounds to awaken and resonate our chakras.

$\backsim$ 6 $\backsim$

The Sacred Vowels

In the Eastern and the Western Mystery schools, the power and sacredness of vowels have been known for thousands of years. Knowledge of the resonation of sacred vowel sounds with the energy centers of the body is said to date back to ancient Egypt.

In Sufism, the mystical path of Islam, vowels are understood as divine attributes. In Kabbalah, the vowel sounds are considered the vibrations of Heaven, while the consonants contain the energy of the Earth. Between the two, communication is possible. Many Kabbalists believe that the true sacred name of God is composed solely of vowel sounds.

It certainly makes sense to us that if an understanding of the chakras dates as far back as the ancient Mystery schools, and an understanding of vowels as sacred sounds also existed at about that same time, then knowledge of how to use the vowels to resonate the chakras most probably existed then as well.

As we discovered in the previous chapter, the *AH* sound is a powerful tool for resonating the heart center. As mentioned, in many traditions the *AH* is believed to be a sacred seed syllable—one of the primordial sounds of manifestation. It is also, simply, a vowel sound. As such, it is a sound that we work with in many different groups; it is easy to sound and transcends any religious taboos.

As noted previously, in his early research, Jonathan found many varied systems of tones and frequencies used by different people to balance and align the chakras. These systems were not necessarily in agreement with each other. Realizing this led to Jonathan's creation of the "Frequency + Intent = Healing" formula.

Jonathan, however, found teachers who utilized vowel sounds to resonate the chakras that were quite similar. It seemed to Jonathan that while there was a substantial difference in the frequencies and tones found in the various systems of chakra resonance, the similarity of the vowel sounds to resonate the chakras needed to be explored. In addition, there was another relationship of sound to the human body that also needed to be examined: the relationship of the human body and potentially the chakras to pitch. Pitch is the subjective term that correlates with frequency; we perceive, for example, the relative "highness" or "lowness" of a sound in terms of its pitch.

Deep bass sounds resonate the lower part of the trunk, mid-range sounds resonate the upper part, and high-pitched sounds resonate the head. Anyone who has ever walked into a dance club with a pounding bass knows that the area around the belly and below will begin to vibrate with the sound of a powerful bass.

Experiencing Pitch

You can experience the relationship of pitch to your body by making some sounds. Find somewhere comfortable to sit where you can make sounds and not be disturbed. This is important because many times it is necessary to focus our attention on the sounds we are creating in order to feel them. It's also good to keep your back as straight as possible whenever you are doing sounding exercises.

Let's experiment for a moment.

Begin by taking some slow deep breaths into your body.

Now very gently make the lowest *OOO* (as in the word "you") sound that you can make. Make this sound three times and notice what you feel. Where did you feel it? You will most naturally feel the sound vibrating in your throat.

Make the *OOO* sound again. What do you notice? Are you aware of the sound vibrating elsewhere in your body?

Some people find it helpful to put their hands gently on their stomach when they make this sound. You may feel a tingling or a slight vibration in your belly area as you make this *OOO* sound. Remember, it doesn't have to be a loud sound—just let it ride gently on your breath; create it as an inwardly directed sound. Many people can feel the *OOO* vibrate lower in their trunk when they do this. Initially, some people may have difficulty feeling anything at all. As we have mentioned before, this is natural. The more you work with sound, the easier it is to feel vibrations in different parts of your body.

Next make a mid-range *AH* sound, perhaps just like the *AH* sound you made in the last chapter. Make this mid-range *AH* sound three times and see what you feel. What do you notice? Where did the sound resonate?

You might want to put your hands lightly on the center of your chest and see if you notice any sensations or vibrations there. You will, of course, notice these vibrations in your throat, but check yourself out to notice the sound in your chest as well.

Finally, make the highest pitched *EEE* sound (as in "me") that you can make. Remember not to strain in any way. What do you notice this time?

If you're a man and you can create a falsetto voice comfortably, please do so. Sometimes, it's helpful to add an *NNN* sound, so that you are toning *NNNEEEE* (like the word "knee"). This nasalizing can be useful in amplifying and bringing the sound into your head.

Lightly touch the sides and top of your skull with your fingers as you are making this sound. Do you feel any vibrations in your head as you do this?

Professional singers, particularly opera and classically trained singers, can testify to the fact that there is a huge difference between a body voice and a head voice, and they are taught how to create both. We mention this simply to show that regardless of the mysticism and esotericism of sound, there are different pitches that resonate different parts of the physical body. They may not be the same pitches for everyone, but low sounds vibrate the lower part of the trunk, mid-range sounds vibrate the mid and upper trunk, and high sounds resonate the head.

Vowels as Mantras

Once Jonathan understood this, he began combining the vowel sounds with different pitches to determine if they resonated different parts of the body. He had found from reading material on speech pathology that different vowel sounds were said to vibrate specific portions of the body naturally. Would combining pitches with these specific vowel sounds amplify this resonance and produce a noticeable effect? Indeed it did. If the different parts of the physical body could be resonated through this combination of vowel sounds and pitches, then perhaps the chakras related to specific parts of the body could also be resonated with these pitches. This idea led to the creation of an exercise called "Vowels as Mantras." In truth, much of this work is based on ancient material that many of Jonathan's colleagues also worked with; he simply clarified certain vowel sounds in relationship to the chakras and popularized this exercise via his writings and recordings.

Before we begin, again, here are a few reminders. It is important when working with self-created sounds to always do them in a comfortable place where you will not be disturbed. Remember to breathe deeply and slowly before, during, and after the sounding. When sounding, make sure you are creating a gentle and comfortable sound and be sure you are not straining your voice in any way. It is not necessary to make loud sounds in order to create effective frequency shifts. As always, remember to be in silence at the completion of the exercise in order for the sound to penetrate, allowing shifts and changes to occur in your subtle bodies down to the physical body.

First Chakra

Begin with an *UH* sound (as in "huh") that is the deepest sound you can make. Focus your attention on the first (root) chakra, located between the genitals and the anus. Visualize the color red at this chakra. Close your eyes while you are making this sound. Focus your attention on the lowest part of your trunk and project your intention so that you visualize the sound resonating between the genitals and the anus. Feel the sound vibrating that area and, as it does, become aware that the energy center associated with this area is also resonating and becoming balanced and aligned through your sounds. Make this *UH* sound seven times.

Second Chakra

Now focus your attention on the second (or sacral) chakra located about three inches below the navel. The vowel sound for this is an *OOO* sound (as in "you"). Orange will complement this visualization. Begin to tone an *OOO* sound, making it a little less deep than the *UH*, and a slightly higher pitch. This sound should be soft and gentle, as should all the sounds in this exercise. Close your eyes and notice where the sound is resonating in your body. Focus your attention on the area of the second chakra and project the sound to this area. As the sound resonates the second chakra, experience this energy center balancing and aligning with the first chakra. Make this *OOO* sound seven times.

Third Chakra

The third chakra, often called the navel chakra, is located around the navel. The sound for this is *OH* (as in "go"). The color yellow will complement your visualization. Begin to tone a very gentle and soft *OH* sound in the mid range of your voice. This should be slightly higher in pitch than the sound for the last chakra. Close your eyes and notice where that sound is resonating in your body. Now focus your attention on the navel and project the sound to this area. As the sound resonates this area, experience this energy center balancing and aligning with the other chakras. Make this *OH* sound seven times.

Fourth Chakra

The vowel sound for the heart (fourth) chakra, located in the middle of the chest, is *AH* (as in "father"). *AH* is often a sound we make when we are in love, and indeed the heart chakra is the center associated with love. If you wish to add a color to complement this sound, green or pink works nicely. Begin to tone a soft and gentle mid-range *AH* sound, higher in pitch than for the last chakra. Become aware of where the sound is resonating in your body. Now focus your attention on the heart chakra and project the sound there. As you resonate the heart center with sound, experience this energy center being balanced and aligned with the other chakras. Make this *AH* sound seven times.

Fifth Chakra

The vowel sound for the throat (fifth) chakra, located at the throat, is *EYE* (as in "I"). A color to complement this sound is light blue. Begin to tone a soft and gentle *EYE* sound, which is still higher in pitch than the sound for the last chakra. Become aware of where the sound is resonating in your body. Now focus your attention on the throat chakra and project sound there. As the sound resonates the throat chakra, experience this energy center balancing and aligning with the other chakras. Make this *EYE* sound seven times.

Sixth Chakra

The vowel sound for the third eye (the sixth chakra), located in

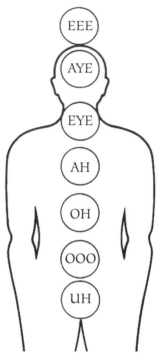

Figure 7 The seven chakras with their related vowels.

the forehead between the eyes and slightly above them, is *AYE* (as in "say"). A color that works well with this sound is indigo. Begin to tone a soft and gentle *AYE* sound higher in pitch than the sound for the last chakra. Close your eyes while making this sound and notice where the sound is resonating in your body. Now focus your attention on this chakra and project the sound to the third eye area. As the sound resonates the third eye, experience this energy center aligning and balancing with your other chakras. Make this *AYE* sound seven times.

Seventh Chakra

The vowel sound for the crown (seventh) chakra, located at the top of the head, is the very highest *EEE* (as in "me") sound that you can create. A color to complement this chakra is purple. Begin to tone the highest *EEE* sound that is possible for you to make. For men, it is often useful to use a falsetto voice to achieve this, but make the sound soft and gentle. Close your eyes and notice where that sound is resonating in your body. Now focus your attention on your crown center and project sound to this area. As your sound resonates the crown chakra, experience this energy center being balanced and aligned with the other chakras. Make this *EEE* sound seven times.

At the completion of this exercise (which takes approximately 20 minutes), remember to maintain a period of silence. You may feel lightheaded, which is to be expected. You have been sounding, resonating, and balancing your chakras. The energy has moved up your spine into your head, and above. During workshops, we tell our participants to take this opportunity of being in silence to have that experience that will be for their highest benefit at this particular moment in their spiritual development. Sit in a state of meditation and enjoy this experience. Allow yourself a good ten to 15 minutes for meditation.

After this meditation, bring yourself slowly back into your body and ground yourself. Do this in two simple steps: (1) Tone a mid-range *AH* sound three times, breathing slowly and bringing the energy down to the heart area; and then (2) tone three of the deepest *UH* sounds, bringing the energy back into the base chakra.

This exercise can take approximately 30 minutes, sometimes an hour if you're having a good meditation. For many people, this is a powerful and transformative experience. This is true not only during the toning, when you're resonating, balancing, and aligning your chakras with sacred sound, but also afterward, while experiencing inner journeys and meditations. In workshops, some people are in a state of bliss once they return to their bodies after their meditations.

This exercise helps make clear the power of sound. Sound can act like a psychoactive substance, altering and enhancing consciousness. However, unlike substances or chemicals that alter consciousness, the wonderful thing about sound is that it is natural and controllable. Sound will only allow you to journey to a place that you are ready to experience. In other words, since it is natural and of your own manifestation, it is safe. The experiences people have are almost always benevolent, blissful, or beautiful. This is the wonder of self-created sacred sound. You do the creation, and wherever you go or whatever you do is guided by your inner wisdom. If you need to stop the experience, open your eyes, take a few breaths, and you're back to normal consciousness.

Of the thousands of people who have worked with us using sacred sound, none have had adverse effects. During workshops, the only complaint we get from people is that we brought them back and grounded them too soon—they were having too much fun! We remind them that they can always return to where they were and whatever they were doing by using the Vowels as Mantras practice.

Give Yourself Time to Assimilate the Experience

Once again, when you do this exercise, especially the first time, allow yourself enough time to enjoy the benefits that accompany this toning practice. Do this in a safe environment where you will not be disturbed. Sitting in a comfortable chair or on the floor is recommended but never in a car or standing up. Allow yourself time after the meditation to relax and integrate the experience once you have grounded yourself. Don't immediately rush to pick up the kids at school or go into that business meeting, particularly the first time you experience this. Just give yourself time. The more you practice Vowels as Mantras, the more you will understand how powerful it is, and how to integrate it into your life.

≈ 7 ≈

The *Bija* Mantras

The word *mantra* is from Sanskrit and may be translated as "thoughts that liberate from samsara, the world of illusions." Mantras also refer to the science of mystic sound and vibration. Mantras are listened to or recited by a practitioner for different purposes: to achieve different states of consciousness, to create resonance with specific attributes of divine energy, or to manifest different qualities, from resonating the chakras to embodying compassion.

Mantras are "words of power." They are found in all the sacred traditions including Judaism and Christianity. The "Hail Mary" and "Amen" in the Christian tradition or the "Shema" and "Shalom" in the Hebrew tradition are the equivalents of mantras, as is any repetition of prayer, chant, or sacred sound. The mantric counterpart in the Islamic Sufi tradition is called the *wazifah*. The prayers, chants, and sacred sounds of the Native Americans and indigenous peoples can also be considered mantras. In fact, there is no spiritual tradition in which the recitation of sacred sound or chants does not occur.

In the Hindu tradition, there are thousands of mantras. Mantras have been studied as a science; each mantra is different, with a unique purpose and intention. Some mantras are designed to empower the reciter with specific powers or *siddhis*. Other mantras are designed to invoke specific energies or deities and unite the reciter with these deities. Still other mantras resonate and activate the chakras of the reciter. The principle of how mantras work is similar to how sound heals.

How Mantras Work

According to Swami Vishnu Devananda in *Meditation and Mantras* (Om Lotus, 1978), "Everything in the universe vibrates on specific wavelengths. These wavelengths can be manipulated. For example, when its pitch is created high enough, a violin note can shatter glass. The various mantras, although equally efficient, vibrate on different wavelengths."

In theory, by repeating a mantra over and over, an individual is able to reattune his resonance (or entrain with the energy of the mantra), so that, ultimately, the use of the mantra causes one to resonate with the particular deity or force with which the mantra is aligned. It is as though mantras are sonic formulas. Just as chemical formulas can create particular elements through the addition of different substances, a mantra can create a specific waveform or sonic energy. By resonating with a deity or force, one takes on the qualities of that deity or force. Thus the use of mantras can bring about union with a god, enlightenment, or perhaps attainment of great powers and abilities *(siddhis)*.

Bijas—Seed Sounds

In this chapter, we will work with a form of mantra designed to balance and align the chakras. The most basic of these mantras is the *bija* mantra. The word *bija* means "seed." These *bijas,* or root sounds, are the simplest linguistic portions of sound, called morphemes.

In Hindu paintings and illustrations, chakras are often depicted as looking like flowers. There are a different number of petals for each flower representing the different chakras. Within the petals of these flowers are squiggly lines that are actually letters of the Sanskrit alphabet. These

Figure 8 The Throat Chakra: around the flower are the whispered *bija* petals. In the center is the chanted *bija*.

letters of the Sanskrit alphabet are the *bijas*. There are 50 letters in this alphabet and different letters are assigned to different chakras.

The Hindu tradition believes that these alphabet letters are sacred and that they compose the fiber of existence. The 50 basic sounds of the *bijas* make up the various wavelengths that create form in the physical world.

The *bijas* are sounded silently or whispered. Within the entire set of *bijas*—the Hindu alphabet—is a subset of sounds; these are particular *bijas* chanted aloud to resonate the chakras. These are the *bija* mantras that we will work with in this chapter.

Note that the 50 letters of Sanskrit are powerful to sound, and for those with an interest in learning them, there are many excellent books on the subject including John Beaulieu's *Music and Sound in the Healing Arts* (Station Hill, 1987) and *Kundalini: Yoga for the West* by Swami Sivananda Radha (Shambhala, 1978). The chanted *bija* mantras are an excellent, easy-to-learn sonic tool that can create transformation and change. We found it simpler to learn to chant seven single-syllable mantras than 50 mantras. We have thus far not found it necessary to work with all 50 *bijas,* but we encourage anyone interested to pursue this.

OM

Let's focus on the most well-known and most often chanted *bija* mantra, *OM.* Undoubtedly, at any given moment, there is someone, somewhere chanting this. The *OM* is considered one of the oldest vocal sounds in existence; many speculate that it has been chanted for untold thousands of years. In the Hindu tradition, it is considered to be the original, primordial sound, the mantra from which the universe and all of creation first manifested.

A Sanskrit word, *OM* is said to be the combination of both the masculine and feminine, the representation of unity. While pronounced *OM* (as in "home"), certain Sanskrit scholars state that it is written as *AUM;* many consider the two words to be interchangeable. *OM* is said to be the sound that contains all sounds; it is the totality of all sounds. Swami Sivananda Radha in *Mantras: Words of Power* (Timeless, 1980) says, "The cosmic sound AUM, or its condensed form, OM, is the origin of all other sound. OM is everything. It is the name of God."

OM may be understood in a number of different ways. One understanding is that *OM*—or its written form, *AUM*—represents attributes of the major trinity of Hindu gods: Brahma, Vishnu, and Shiva. The sounding of the "A" represents the energy of Brahma, the creator and the creational process. The middle portion of the sound, the "U," represents the energy of Vishnu, the preserver, and relates to the maintenance and preservation of what has been created. The final "M" represents the energy of Shiva, the transformer, and relates to the vital transformational energy to shift and change that which has been created and preserved.

Another understanding of the *OM* or *AUM* is that the "A" represents the physical plane, the "U" the mental and astral planes, and the "M" all that is beyond the reach of the intellect. *OM* or *AUM* is the initial sylla-ble that begins almost all mantras. Thus *OM* represents the infinite, the One Mind, the all-embracing consciousness, the essence of existence.

In Tibetan Buddhism, the *OM (AUM)* represents different aspects of the trinity of the Body, Speech, and Mind of the Buddha. The "A" represents the Body, the "U" represents Speech, and the "M" repre-sents the Mind. Sounding the *AUM* in this manner puts one in reso-nance with these qualities.

OM can, through intent, become a multipurpose mantra capable of resonating and aligning all the chakras and cleansing imbalanced energies and purifying self. Intoned with sincerity and devotion, vocalization of the *OM* can put the chanter in touch with the source of all creation, providing a bridge between the spiritual and physical dimensions and opening the way for inspirational contact with higher realms and beings.

OM as a sound symbolizes the supreme source, and, to many, the sound of *OM* is synonymous with the energy of peace. *OM* is the root of many sacred words of different languages including our western "Amen" and the Hebrew "Shalom," which has many meanings including "peace." The *OM* initiates peace and tranquility when it is listened to, and particularly when it is chanted.

Of course, it is not necessary to know this about the *OM* before you chant it, but we thought some knowledge of the *OM* would be of inter-est. This material is merely a synthesis and summary of information about the *OM*. One could write a book about this sound.

Within all systems of sound, there seem to be many variations, including chanting the *bija* mantras. In many of the more traditional versions, there is, in fact, no chanted *bija* for the crown center; instead, one meditates on the silence of this chakra (the silent or whispered *bijas*). However, in our work we have found the following version that uses seven chanted *bija* mantras—one *bija* for each chakra—to be extremely effective for chakra resonance. We have successfully used this version of seven chanted *bijas,* as have many others, including Dr. Deepak Chopra.

The other *bija* mantras are: *LAM, VAM, RAM, YAM, HAM,* and *SHAM.* These are used, respectively, for the first through sixth chakras, with *OM (AUM)* being used for the seventh chakra. Before we begin our exercise with the *bija* mantras, we would like to cover pronunciation of these sounds and what we believe may be the major vibrational focus with regard to these sounds.

Proper Pronunciation of *Bijas*

Many people ask if there is a correct pronunciation for the *OM.* Is it *OM* or *AUM,* or something else entirely? In reality, there does not seem to be one exact, correct pronunciation. Depending on the country, language, and dialect, the *OM* can be pronounced *AUM, UM, UNG, ANG,* and *ONG,* among other pronunciations. The *OM* may also be chanted as a three-syllable word *AUM* (pronounced as *AH–OH–MMM*). Yet the resonance and effects of this mantra seem to be similar despite varied differences in pronunciation. Much depends, of course, on the intention of the person creating the sound.

This is true about the other *bija* mantras as well. *LAM, VAM, RAM, YAM, HAM,* and *SHAM* all have variation in their soundings. *LAM* can be pronounced *LUM, LANG* (nasalizing the "ng" sound), or *LUNG.* The same variations apply to the other sounds. We have not found much difference with regard to the effect of the sounds once they are made. What does seem to be important is that, for example, if you choose to pronounce *LAM* as *LANG,* then pronounce all the other *bija* mantras similarly: Thus *VAM* is *VANG* and not pronounced as *VAM, VUM,* or *VUNG; RAM* is pronounced *RANG;* and so on.

For the *bija* mantra exercise, we will pronounce the *bija* mantras as they are spelled, pronouncing the "A" as *AH* (as in "father") and pronouncing each letter as in *LL-AH-MM* for *LAM.* Later, when we give instructions for this exercise, we also give you the phonetic pronunciation of the *bija* mantra.

Before we begin this exercise we want to affirm the power of the *bija* mantras. These sounds are extremely old and have been effectively used for thousands of years by millions of people to resonate their chakras. They have been tried and proven. We have personally had enormous success working with the *bija* mantras in our workshops.

Elongating the Consonants

From a linguistic view, we have observed that the only difference between these *bija* mantras seems to be the consonant at the beginning of the sound. Other than that, they are basically the same. Therefore it appears to us that the differentiating power of the *bija* mantras may be this beginning consonant. We have spoken to a number of practitioners of *bija* mantras who agree with us. When you chant these mantras, elongate the beginning consonant. When we chant these seed syllables, at least one third of the sound (sometimes even half of our breath, and therefore of the sound) is devoted to creating this first consonant.

With *LAM,* for example, if it takes eight seconds to sound the entire word, three or four of those seconds are occupied making the *LLLL* sound while the remaining four seconds are equally split between the *AH* and the *MM* sounds. If we were to write the pronunciation phonetically it would be something like *LLLLLLLL-AAAH-MMMM.*

Of course, you will find schools and teachers who will tell you that (1) the only correct pronunciation of *LAM* is *LANG;* or (2) the emphasis should be on the last "ng" sound so that it should be pronounced *L-AH-NNNNNNNGGGGGG.* When sounding the *bija* mantras, use what works effectively for you. If you like, try our pronunciation first and then experiment with the others; or if you are drawn to another pronunciation, use that. Once again, fluidity is the key we emphasize here.

There are many different pitch variations that can be applied when you sound the *bija* mantras. In later chapters, we will experiment with them (as we will also experiment with pitch variations using the sacred vowels). However, at this time, for this exercise, we suggest you find a note that feels comfortable, and then sound each *bija* mantra on this note.

In India, where millions chant the *bijas* daily, a majority of reciters chant them in a monotone, never changing their pitch. In the previous chapter, when experimenting with the sacred vowels, we changed pitch to feel the resonance in our bodies and chakras. In this chapter, to demonstrate another aspect of chakra resonance, we will stay on the same pitch. Once you feel like experimenting, please try other variations. Learning to be fluid with sound is an important part of tantra and of understanding the power of sound.

We want to remind you again of the importance when working with self-created sounds to find a comfortable place where you will not be disturbed. Remember to breathe deeply and slowly before, during, and after the sounding. When sounding, make sure you are creating a gentle and comfortable sound, and be sure you are not straining your voice in any way. As always, it is not necessary to make loud sounds in order to create effective frequency shifts, and be in silence when the exercise is complete.

Bija Mantra Exercise

First *Bija*

We begin with the root chakra and the mantra *LAM*. Sound the mantra, *LLLLLLL-AAAH-MMMM*, using a comfortable pitch. Focus your attention on the base chakra, located in the perineum between the genitals and anus. If you want to add a color visualization to this exercise, use the color red. Close your eyes while making this sound. Focus your attention on the lowest part of your trunk and project your intention so that you visualize the sound resonating in the root chakra. Feel the sound vibrating this area and, as it does, become aware that this energy center is now resonating, becoming balanced and aligned through sacred sound. Make the *LAM* sound seven times.

Second *Bija*

Now focus your attention on the second chakra located about three inches below the navel. The *bija* mantra for this chakra is *VAM* (pronounced *VVVVVVV-AAAH-MMMM*). A color that will complement your visualization for this chakra is orange. Begin to sound the *VAM* in a comfortable pitch. Close your eyes and notice where the sound is resonating in your body. Now focus your attention on the second chakra and project the sound there. As the sound resonates the second chakra, experience this energy center becoming balanced and aligned with the previous chakra. Make the *VAM* sound seven times.

Third *Bija*

The *bija* mantra for the third chakra, located at the navel, is *RAM* (pronounced *RRRRRRR-AAAH-MMMM*). Yellow will complement your visualization. Begin to tone a very gentle and soft *RAM*. Notice where this sound is resonating in your body. Now focus your attention on this third chakra, and project the sound there. As the sound resonates this area, experience this energy center balancing and aligning with the other chakras. Chant the *RAM* sound seven times.

Fourth *Bija*

The *bija* mantra for the fourth chakra, the heart center located in the middle of the chest, is *YAM*. If you wish to add a color to complement this sound, use green. We find it easiest to add an *EEE* sound before the Y in order to elongate the Y, so that the pronunciation is *EEEEEE-YAAH-MMMM*. Begin to tone this in the same comfortable way that you have been using. Notice where the sound is resonating in your body. Now focus your attention on the heart chakra and project the sound there. As you resonate the heart center with sound, experience this energy center balancing and aligning with the other chakras. Chant the *YAM* sound seven times.

Fifth *Bija*

Now focus your attention on the fifth chakra, located at the throat. The *bija* mantra for this chakra is *HAM*. A color to complement this sound is sky blue. We find that it's sometimes a bit difficult to make an elongated H sound unless it is an aspirate H that is sounded very softly, so that the *HHH* almost rides at first on the breath and then becomes slightly louder. It is pronounced *HHHHHH-AAAH-MMMM*. Begin to tone the *HAM* mantra. Notice where the sound is resonating in your body. Now focus your attention on the throat chakra and project sound there. As the sound resonates the throat chakra, experience this energy center balancing and aligning with the other chakras. Make the *HAM* sound seven times.

Sixth *Bija*

Now focus your attention on the sixth chakra, often called the third eye, located on the forehead midway between the eyes and slightly above. The *bija* mantra for this chakra is *SHAM*. We pronounce this mantras as *SSSSHHH-AAAH-MMMM*. A color that works well with this chakra is indigo. Begin to tone that same comfortable note you have been using throughout this exercise. Close your eyes while making this sound and become aware of where that sound is resonating in your body. Now focus your attention on this chakra and project the sound to that area. As the sound resonates the third eye, experience this energy center aligning and balancing with your other chakras. Make the *SHAM* sound seven times.

Seventh *Bija*

The *bija* mantra for the crown chakra, located at the top of the head, is *OM*. For use in this exercise we simply pronounce it as *OOOOOHHH-MMMM*. A color that is used here is purple. Begin to tone the *OM* mantra in a comfortable voice. Close your eyes and notice where this sound is resonating in your body. Now focus your attention on your crown center and begin to project sound there. As the sound resonates the crown chakra, experience this energy center being balanced and aligned with all the other chakras. Chant the *OM* mantra seven times.

Now be in silence.

When you feel complete with your meditation, take as much time as you need to feel grounded.

As with the previous sound exercise (Vowels as Mantras), the *Bija* Mantra exercise takes approximately 20 minutes. At the end of it, you may feel lightheaded. We suggest that you take this opportunity to sit in silence as long as you'd like, and have the experience that is for your highest benefit at this particular moment in your spiritual development. Sit in a state of meditation and enjoy this experience. You have been sounding, resonating, and

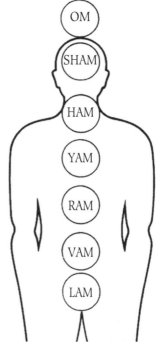

Figure 9 Diagram of the *bija* mantras in relation to the seven chakras.

balancing your chakras as the energy has moved up your spine and into your head, and above. Allow yourself a good ten to 15 minutes for this meditation and then be sure to ground yourself thoroughly.

As with our experience with vowels in the last chapter, this *bija* mantra exercise with meditation and all can take from a half-hour to an hour to complete. It can be a powerful and transformative experience.

When you do this exercise with the *bija* mantras, allow yourself enough time to enjoy the benefits that accompany it. This is especially true the first time you do it. Do this in a safe environment where you will not be disturbed, allowing yourself enough time after the meditation to relax and integrate the experience once you have grounded yourself.

In the next section of *Tantra of Sound* we present more sound exercises and experiences that you can use by yourself or share with a partner. These sounds, and the way you are able to resonate with them using your intent and visualization, are the basis of many traditional tantric exercises. Familiarity with them will enhance your health and consciousness, as well as assisting with the other exercises in this book. Practice these ancient sacred sounds wholeheartedly, and you will definitely notice a difference.

Part III

Practice with a Partner

❧ 8 ❧

Overall Purpose

As we begin this next section, which focuses on sound exercises with a partner, it is important to first ask this question: What is your purpose and intention for engaging in sound activities with another person?

Is it to meditate together and resonate your consciousness together? Is it to reach deeper emotional levels and achieve empathic rapport with one another? Do you want to use these activities as a counseling tool to enhance communication, and go into deeper levels of understanding together? Do you desire to enhance the physical resonance you have with another, and use these vibratory tools to heighten your exploration of sacred love through the act of sex? Are you seeking to expand the love, health, and vitality you have with your partner, or to generate compassion together for both personal and planetary healing?

There is no right or wrong answer to these questions. Everyone is

81

unique and different, and every relationship is unique and different. What is so wonderful about sound is that it can assist and enhance every aspect of relationship, from co-meditation to shifting anger to making love. Sound can help you achieve each one of the elements implied in the questions, as well as much more. Whatever your reasons for learning this material, we are grateful that you are joining us on this journey through sound, intimacy, and partnership.

We must offer a caution: Sound is a profound tool for transformation—it will change you. That is a fact. As we've mentioned in previous chapters, while sound will only take you to places that you are ready for, your experiences with sound will deepen your relationship with your partner and yourself.

In fact, if you have been practicing the exercises from the previous chapters, you have probably already experienced this. Therefore it is likely you are a different person now from who you were before you began working with self-created sound. And if you did not do those exercises and have skipped to this section, the following information, in particular, is for you.

Know Thyself

Over the gates of Delphi in Greece, the sacred spot where the oracle gave divine messages to the Pythia, or priestess, it read, "Know Thyself!" This concept of "Know Thyself" is, of course, not restricted to the teachings of ancient Greece; there is not a philosopher or spiritual teacher that we can think of who has not advised similar awareness in each pupil. Whether one is undergoing a spiritual quest or psychological journey, or simply becoming a better person, one of the primary steps necessary is becoming better acquainted with oneself. Understanding ourselves at a deep level is paramount, and it is not an easy thing to do. While it takes work and commitment, it is definitely possible. Self-acceptance and self-love are the ultimate goals in working toward knowing thyself. The power of sound can greatly assist this process.

When we speak of knowing ourselves, we are not talking about how we view ourselves in terms of career, job, and family, or how we may appear to the outside world. Whether you're a doctor, lawyer, shaman, or mother, these are still external descriptions of how the world sees you and how you may see yourself. Certainly, these descriptions can tell us a great deal about how we might occupy our thoughts and time with regard to the outside world, but they tell us little about our true essence and our connection with the web of life.

What emotions flow in and out of our lives? How aware are we of them? Do we feel happy, sad, scared, or confused? Do we long for peace, joy, or rest? Are you a 13-year-old boy encased in the body of a 40-year-old man? Are you a beam of light shrouded in the dark? By focusing ourselves on a deeper level, it's possible to receive insights that can help us know and understand ourselves. Through knowing ourselves, we can achieve levels of self-acceptance and inner peace that many have only dreamed of.

As we take a deeper look into our emotions and process our feelings, we can begin to access ways of experiencing intimacy and a deeper connection with all of life. It is through understanding and experiencing self-acceptance and self-love that we can share this love with others. By discovering how to love ourselves, we can then know how to love others.

Using sound is a valuable tool for helping us open up to these deeper levels of life. Sound coupled with intention can help dissolve blockages that may be holding us back and keeping us from knowing ourselves and loving others. It is through understanding and experiencing our own connection with life through the power of sound that profound shifts and changes can occur.

The Activating Agent of Tantra

When you make sounds by yourself and experience the silence after the sound, you most likely reach a stillness within you. In that stillness, perhaps an aspect of yourself may be revealed to you. Sound can do that because sound is the activating agent of tantra, the web that unites all things. Tantra is the field of unity between us—the "Force" that we so fondly remember from *Star Wars*. As you begin to know and trust this field of unity, you begin to know and trust not only yourself, but your interconnectedness with all things.

As you understand this interconnectedness, you can begin the process of surrender not only to yourself, but also to the divine aspect within all of us. Using sound therapeutically, people can begin to relinquish aspects of control they may have had, surrendering this control to a higher force. Once you realize the existence of tantra, the web of life, you know there is more going on than meets the eye. You may be a cocreator of reality, but you are not *the* creator.

Your actions and reactions are interdependent with countless other actions and reactions over which you have no control and of which you have little understanding. Such a realization can take a burden off those who feel a need to control every aspect of life. Not only is this not possible, it is an illusion and is not useful. Releasing such issues frees us in many ways—in body, in mind, and in spirit. Since sound has the extraordinary ability to shift and change us on many levels, you may begin to uncover an understanding about love and compassion that may not have been in your consciousness when you began your journey with tantra of sound.

Integrating Masculine and Feminine Energy

Most frequently in the tantric traditions, one's partner is actually an internalized being, a sexual counterpart of the divine aspect of ourselves. If you are a man, this internalized being is a woman; and vice versa. Through tantric activities such as those presented in this book, using sound individuals can unite the male and female aspects of themselves in meditations, becoming one with the divine and with the essence of the universe and with divine beings such as Jesus and Mary Magdalene, Shiva and Shakti, Avalokitesvara and Tara, or any of the countless divine male/female energy forms found in other traditions. Regardless of your belief system, there are divine models of male and female energy just waiting to work with you to achieve balance and higher consciousness.

∽ 9 ∾

Using Vowel Sounds
with a Partner

The previous chapters involved working with sound by yourself. In those chapters we used two systems of chakra resonance—sacred vowels and the *bija* mantras. In this section, we will use these two again but with a partner. These exercises provide simple, effective methods of achieving vibratory resonance with another person. In these new chapters we offer variations on the exercises you have already experienced. These can present new insights into sound and tantra beneficial to you and your partner. The concept of using sound to resonate the chakras remains the same.

In chapter 6, we suggested that when you work individually with the Vowels as Mantras exercise, you go from the lowest sound you can make for the first chakra to the highest sound you can make for the seventh chakra. The potential in this initial form is extraordinary, so we use it again while sounding with a partner.

You no doubt have found by now (due to your diligent practice with the previous exercises) that the more you practiced, the more easily and effectively you experienced the resonances of your body and chakras. You undoubtedly have experienced moving a pitch slightly up, or down, while resonating a particular chakra. You may also have found that the resonance changed and discovered that the pitch for any given chakra is not static. In fact, the resonance shifts depending on any number of elements, including our physical, emotional, and mental activities before and after the exercise.

Matching Pitch with a Partner

The exercise of Vowels as Mantras done with a partner can begin to enhance your connection to each other. When you do this exercise with a partner, rather than having one person lead with their tone and one person match, begin in an egalitarian manner—that is, with both people finding a comfortable pitch—and then work with that pitch until you match each other comfortably.

This way you'll both have an equal place to start at the beginning of the exercise, and matching each other's pitch will assist the experience of resonating your chakras together. The basic idea here is simply to match each other's pitch as closely as possible. It does not matter what note you use as long as you both feel comfortable making the sound together. This is a huge step for many people, not only in experiencing the tantra of sound, but in developing intimacy.

The Wounded Singer

Many of us are wounded singers, having experienced some form of rejection when we sang in public, whether it was being told to go out for track when we tried out for the school choir, or being laughed at by family members if we started singing a song. No doubt, many of you reading this will be able to relate to being a wounded singer, someone who is positive they cannot sing. The good news is that the sound exercises in this book have nothing to do with singing.

Please be assured, we know that sounding with a partner can initially be a frightening experience, particularly if you have had some of these wounding experiences. Because of this, it's important to honor that sounding with a partner requires levels of trust and nonjudgment. One thing that can initially help this feeling is to be as good-humored as possible with each other, and to give each other a break—laughing is great! Remember, there are no rules, no right or wrong sounds. Give yourself permission to be silly and playful as you're getting started and remember it's impossible to make a wrong sound.

If you can find a tone to sound together that feels mildly comfortable for you both—a tone that you are generating with the energy of compassion and love—this will be a good beginning to resonate together. We suggest that unless you are the spiritual equivalent of Sonny and Cher, begin practicing the exercise of Vowels as Mantras using the same tone for each chakra, sounding one single note for all of the chakras.

This is called singing in monotone. It's an effective, easy, and simple sonic exercise to experience. It is an ancient and noble method of sacred chanting, and one we strongly suggest if this is the first time you and your partner have endeavored to sound together. After you have experienced this a couple of times and you feel comfortable sounding together, you can begin doing more advanced variations of this exercise.

Incidentally, we also suggest to you that if you find it difficult, threatening, or impossible to match each other's pitch, practice the exercises anyway. We have at times observed the fear factor of sounding with another being so great that people will automatically sing out of tune, even when this is actually more difficult to do than singing in tune. How? Why? We aren't sure, but we believe it may have something to do with unconsciously hearing that inner voice of the wounded singer that may still need a little tender healing.

Frequently, we've found that people who consider themselves tone deaf can often match the pitch of someone else, until they start thinking about it. They'll be toning along fine with another person, then someone says something about matching pitch, or another suggestion that triggers the "I can't sing" button. Suddenly, the two people who moments before were singing along beautifully are now sounding disharmonious.

Even if you and your partner feel as though you sound like a pair of howling coyotes—in certain indigenous traditions this is considered quite good!—continue sounding. Believe that once you've gotten over your fear and allowed yourself to feel comfortable sounding with another person, your pitch-matching problems will be over. After that, the sky's the limit! You'll both be able, if you like, to do much more challenging variations of this exercise.

The Out-of-Tune Angel

Here's a quick story that we're guided to share. We trust it will assist you as you're developing your sound work.

Once upon a time, Shamael, Master of Heavenly Song and Director of the Divine Choir, found it necessary to find a replacement for one of the angels who was leaving the choir. The angel had apparently done enough "hosannas" or whatever, and was now going to engage in another equally important activity, but this was never revealed. What was revealed was that there would now be an opening in the Divine Choir for another angelic voice; so naturally they had tryouts to fill the position.

There were angels of all varieties (and believe us—angels come in many varieties). It is written that for each blade of grass growing, there is an angel helping it grow. So you can imagine the immense number of angels that could potentially fill the position. Most of the angels who came for the tryouts thought their abilities best suited for the position. An angel told Shamael, "I can sing the sun up in the morning!" The angel then made an incredible tone and indeed the sun came up. Another angel told Shamael, "I can sing the stars out at night," and indeed this angel did exactly that. On and on, the angels came, each with a seemingly greater gift and power to use sound as a magnificent manifestation of the creator.

Then came this little angel who made a sound, and it was not much. In fact, it was pretty bleak. If some of the other angels had earth-shattering roars, this little angel had more of a squeak. Its voice was hopelessly weak and out of tune. In fact, if there were such a thing as snickering in the angelic realm (which, of course, there is not), the tryouts for the Divine Choir would have been filled with these sounds.

Then, at the end of the day (which, naturally, in the heavenly realms could have easily been a millennium), the angels all went back to their current positions to await the decision. Remember, there was room for only one angel.

The next day the angels all came back and reverentially waited to hear which one had been accepted. Shamael made his announcement and . . . well, we think a lot of you guessed it. The new position in the Divine Choir went to the little angel with the very out-of-tune voice. The other angels were in a quandary, and if disbelief existed in the angelic realms (which, of course, it does not), you would have heard many groans and shouts of opposition: "But . . . but . . . I can sing the sun up in the morning," or "But I can sing the tides from the ocean," and so forth.

Shamael, with his knowing, loving wisdom (for after all, Shamael is second only to the Divine Creator itself in terms of his extraordinarily omniscient compassion and kindness), nodded his head, knowing the thoughts of these other angels. Then he said, "The Divine Choir encircles the Holy of Holies, singing praises of love and joy to the Creator throughout time. Therefore the position that is open in this choir is not one of sonic power or ability. It is one of love. And as I listened to all of you make your extraordinary sounds yesterday, there was one with whom the energy of love was greatest and most abundant." Shamael spread his hands to the little angel with the out-of-tune voice. "And it is this beloved being whom the Creator wishes to have most dearly in the Divine Choir. So welcome!"

Sounding Together with Nonjudgment and Compassion

Perhaps as an aside, we should tell you how this story developed. We were taking part in a sonic meditation with other people around the world, sounding a prayer for peace for five minutes at a specific time. What a beautiful idea. We eagerly engaged in this activity. It was indeed a beautiful experience—at least for the first minute or so, until Jonathan realized that Andi was not matching his note and that we were out of tune. He became frustrated and upset, and he soon stopped making any sound, depressed because he believed our out-of-tune sounds were not assisting the world. Andi, being very empathic, picked up Jonathan's energy and stopped making sound as well, feeling embarrassed and upset. We both sat in meditation, attempting to project the energy of peace onto the planet, but it was difficult. We had both momentarily become wounded singers again!

Then, during our meditation, Shamael told Jonathan the story of "The Out-of-Tune Angel." When Jonathan opened his eyes again and looked at Andi, he realized how wrong and judgmental he had been. With her compassion, Andi forgave Jonathan, and with his compassion, Jonathan was able to forgive himself. For he knew that while Andi's voice might have been out of tune at the time, the love that she generated in her sound was extraordinary. That is what each and every sound exercise in this book is all about: love! It is about intention and vibration, and most certainly not about the necessity of having a skilled and beautiful voice. It's about acceptance and nonjudgment.

We have never publicly shared this story before, but we trust you will find it useful. For those engaged in professional singing careers and who can hit celestial harmonies during this exercise, we salute you. And for those who cannot, we ask you to bring to mind with love and acceptance the story of "The Out-of-Tune Angel." Incidentally, once Jonathan received this story and understood its meaning, he and Andi began to sing more and more in tune. Now, we often sing as one.

Sound the Major Scale

One variation of using tone in the Vowels as Mantras exercise involves using a major scale to sound the chakras. After you have found your matching pitch, you might use a diatonic scale in the key of C. Put another way, you begin with the note C for the first chakra, the note D for the second chakra, E for the third chakra, F for the fourth chakra, G for the fifth chakra, A for the sixth chakra, and B for the seventh chakra. These are the white notes on a piano, going note by note up the piano, starting from the note C.

For those claiming no musical knowledge or ability and finding this difficult, do not worry. Try using the good old "Do, re, mi, fa, sol, la, ti, do" scale from the movie *The Sound of Music*. Remember the "Doe, a deer, a female deer" song? We have all heard the sound of instruments going up the seven steps of the major scale innumerable

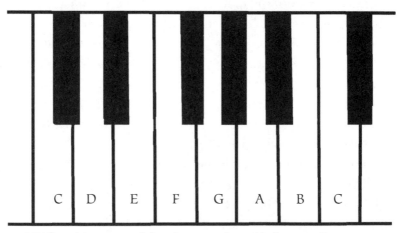

Figure 10 The white notes of the piano starting with the note C.

times in our lives, so it's a simple and familiar scale, built into your sonic memory. Even so, here are some hints for those who consider themselves musically challenged.

We have found that, for many, going up the major scale enhances the ability to feel the sound resonating in the chakras. The C-major scale, represented by the white keys on the piano, is easiest, particularly for people who have a keyboard in their home. However, starting in the key of C is not mandatory. You can start on any note that feels comfortable, particularly if you can go up seven steps together. If it turns out you can sound together using a scale that is different from this major scale, that's fine, too.

When Jonathan first began researching the different systems of using sound to resonate the chakras, he found many different musical scales used by various practitioners. So if you're using a minor augmented flatted seventh scale (we're just making up a name now), or whatever, it's perfectly fine. What's important is that you resonate together and enjoy this experience together. That's the true focus, not the musical scale.

The Magic of Monotone

As previously stated, it's fine if you sing the vowel sounds in monotone, as you did with the *bija* mantras. In fact, for beginners, this is preferred. Monotone means using one note, that is, the same note for each chakra as you're sounding each different vowel sound. This works well. In fact, there are people (with incredible musical knowledge and ability) who find using one note for all the chakras more effective than going up a scale. Why? It probably has to do with harmonics.

Harmonics are sounds within sounds that make up the texture of tone. They are, in fact, the components that create the timbre or tone color of sound. Just as a prism held up to the sunlight displays the colors of the rainbow, harmonics can be called the colors of sound. Each vowel sound has a different set of stressed harmonics (called "formants"). These harmonics go up in pitch as you sing the vowel sounds. You may not be able to hear the changes in harmonics, but on a subtle level, they are occurring and affecting your chakras. This is why doing Vowels as Mantras on a single note works. For those seeking more information about harmonics, we refer you to Jonathan's book *Healing Sounds: The Power of Harmonics.*

Different Methods of Sounding the Chakras

We have now presented you with several different methods for sounding the seven chakras, beginning with the root chakra and moving up to the crown chakra. Here is a review of the methods:

• Sound the vowels from the deepest note to the highest note, as presented in chapter 6.

• Sound the vowels using the C-major scale going from C to D to E to F to G to A to B.

• Sound the vowels using a seven-note major scale starting on whatever note you want.

• Sound the vowels with whatever scale or combination of notes you find comfortable.

• Sound the vowels on a single note, singing monotone (the same note for each vowel sound), and matching each other's pitch.

• Sound the vowels on a single note, singing monotone (the same note for each vowel sound), and not matching each other's pitch.

These are six variations that you can try. Experiment with them and enjoy the process. Anybody can work with these variations, even those of you wounded singers who have been told you are tone-deaf. We do not, incidentally, believe in that concept; no one is tone-deaf. Everyone can learn to sing in tune or match notes. Many of us have powerful belief systems engrained in our psyches that have convinced us that we cannot sing. These beliefs are false messages we have received along the way, and once we can let them go, the blockages begin to dissipate, and we begin to feel our ability to tone and the true power of our voice.

Through practice and experience, we believe that these negative thought forms dissolve, bringing with this dissolution the self-empowerment of using sound as a healing and transformative tool. What matters most is your intention and the loving acceptance of each other, no matter what sounds you are making. We cannot stress this point enough. Even if you and your partner cannot match each other's note (or at least believe you are not matching the note), that doesn't matter.

Remember, it's "Frequency + Intent = Healing."

And "Visualization + Vocalization = Manifestation."

If you're making a vowel sound and focusing your intention on a chakra, that's enough. That's all it takes. It's that simple. It can be interesting and fun to do this exercise using any of the six methods suggested. We know that some of you will get a C tuning fork and begin your resonance together using the second method, and others will find your own vibratory pitch and resonate together using your method of choice. Simply feel comfortable and relaxed while you're sounding a tone with your partner. That's all it takes to do the Vowels as Mantras with Partner exercise.

Purpose and Position

Before we give the instructions on how to do the Vowels as Mantras with Partner exercise, we'd like to suggest some focused purposes for it. Basically, you and your partner will be sounding and resonating your chakras together. This creates a vibratory matching

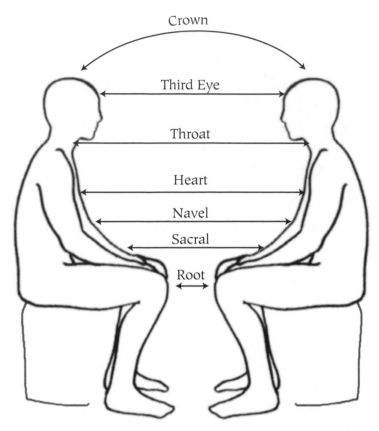

Figure 11 Projecting the energy from your chakras.

frequency (called a sympathetic resonance) between the two of you. This resonance begins to put your bodies, minds, and spirits in harmony.

Usually, we do this exercise while sitting comfortably in chairs facing each other. We are often only a few inches away from each other with our knees almost touching. You can also do this sitting side by side or with your backs against each other, although the ideal way is to face each other if possible. There are many variants of even the positions for doing this exercise.

There is such variety of posture that our recommendation is to do what feels the most comfortable. You can sit in chairs, sit on the floor, or sit in the traditional lotus posture used by yogis and their students.

We do, however, suggest that you do these exercises with your spine as straight as possible. Being hunched over or having your spine distorted in some fashion not only constricts the natural pathways of breath (and therefore of sound), but also seems to interrupt the flow of energy up the spine.

Additional Enhancement

Doing the Vowels as Mantras exercise with another person, sounding together while projecting intentionalized sound, you will create a resonance between you—without doing anything else. Here, however, are some additional ways to enhance the exercise:

• As you focus your intention of balancing and aligning your chakras, also set the intention of balancing and aligning your partner's chakras.

• While focusing this intention, visualize the energy going from your chakras to your partner's (and vice versa). Become aware that your energy is also helping to balance and align your partner's chakras and is connecting you in a deep and intimate way.

• As you focus your intentionalized sound and visualization, add the feeling of appreciation and love to the energy you are projecting. Love can be projected from each and every chakra and can amplify the tantric energy with which you are working.

As always, it is important when working with self-created sounds to do them in a comfortable place where you will not be disturbed. Additionally, remember to breathe deeply and slowly before, during, and after the sounding. When sounding, make sure you are creating a gentle and comfortable sound, and be sure you are not straining your voice in any way. Remember, it is not necessary to make loud sounds in order to create effective frequency shifting. Also remember to be in silence after the exercise.

Vowels as Mantras with Partner Exercise

First Chakra

Begin together with an *UH* sound (as in "huh"). Focus your attention on your first (or root) chakra, located between the genitals and the anus. If you would like to add a color visualization to this chakra, use the color red. You may close your eyes while making this sound or, bet-

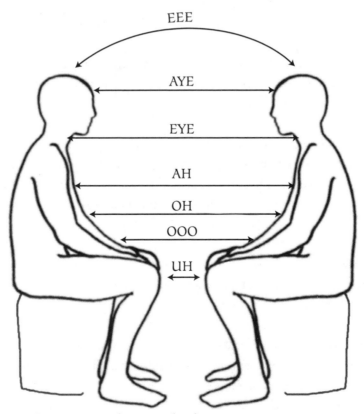

Figure 12 Projecting vowels into each other.

ter yet, look into your partner's eyes. Focus your attention on the lowest part of your trunk and project your intention so that you visualize the sound as resonating at the root chakra.

Feel the sound vibrating and resonating this area. Become aware that the energy center associated with this area is also resonating and becoming balanced and aligned through sacred sound. Project this balanced energy from your root chakra into your partner's root chakra. Experience the giving and receiving of this energy to and from each other. Make this *UH* sound together seven times.

Second Chakra

Now focus your attention on the second (or sacral) chakra located about three inches below the navel. The vowel sound for this chakra is an *OOO* sound (as in "you"). A color that will complement your visualization for this sound is orange. Begin to tone an *OOO* together. Now focus your attention on the area of the second chakra and project the sound there. As the sound resonates the second chakra, experience this energy center as being balanced and aligned with the first chakra. Project this balanced energy from your sacral chakra into your partner's sacral chakra. Experience the giving and receiving of this energy to and from each other. Make this *OOO* sound together seven times.

Third Chakra

The sound for the third (or navel) chakra, located around the navel and slightly above it, is pronounced *OH* (as in "go"). Yellow will complement your visualization. Begin to tone together a very gentle and soft *OH* sound. Focus your attention on the navel area and project the sound there. As the sound resonates this area, experience this energy center balancing and aligning with the other chakras. Project the balanced energy from your third chakra into your partner's third chakra. Experience the giving and receiving of this energy to and from each other. Make this *OH* sound together seven times.

Fourth Chakra

The vowel sound for the fourth (or heart) chakra, located in the middle of the chest, is *AH* (as in "father"). If you wish to add a color to complement this sound, use green. Begin to tone together a soft and gentle mid-range *AH* sound and, as you focus your attention on the heart chakra, project the sound there. As you resonate the heart center with sound, experience this energy center balancing and aligning with the other chakras. Project the balanced energy from your heart chakra into your partner's heart chakra. Experience the giving and receiving of this energy to and from each other. Make this *AH* sound together seven times.

Fifth Chakra

The vowel sound for the fifth (or throat) chakra is *EYE* (as in "I"). A color to complement this sound is sky blue. Begin to tone together a gentle *EYE* sound, and as you focus your attention on your throat chakra, project the sound there. As the sound resonates the throat chakra, experience this energy center balancing and aligning with the other chakras. Project the balanced energy from your throat center into your partner's throat center. Experience the giving and receiving of this energy to and from each other. Make this *EYE* sound together seven times.

Sixth Chakra

The vowel sound for the sixth chakra (or third eye), located on the forehead between the eyes and slightly above, is *AYE* (as in "say"). A color that works well with this sound is indigo. Begin to tone together a soft and gentle *AYE*. Look into your partner's eyes and become aware that, as you focus your attention on this chakra and project the sound to that area, the sound is resonating the third eye and aligning and balancing this energy center with your other chakras. Project the balanced energy from your third eye into your partner's third eye. Experience the giving and receiving of this energy to and from each other. Make this *AYE* sound together seven times.

Seventh Chakra

The vowel sound for the seventh (or crown) chakra, located at the top of the head, is the *EEE* sound (as in "me"). A color that is used here is purple. Begin to tone together a gentle *EEE* sound and as you do, close your eyes, projecting this sound to your crown center. Become aware that this sound is resonating the crown chakra, balancing and aligning this center with the other energy centers. Project the balanced energy from your crown chakra into your partner's crown chakra. Experience the giving and receiving of this energy to and from each other. Make this *EEE* sound together seven times.

Now be in silence.

The sounding part of this exercise takes approximately 20 minutes to complete. As always, it's the time of silence after the sounding that creates the most frequency shifts. You will no doubt feel light-headed after the exercise. After this experience, we strongly recommend that you take some time—perhaps ten minutes or more—to sit in the silence before doing anything else.

What you do during and after this exercise is, of course, dependent on what your initial purpose was for doing this exercise together. No doubt, you will experience a deep connection with your partner. How that connection manifests is up to you. You may be in a deep state of appreciation and love with each other. You might (when you return to the land of the verbal) begin a deep, heartfelt communication that transcends anything you've previously experienced. You might just lie down, hold each other, and explore the spiritual realms together. You might indulge in a sensual exploration of the physical as your merged energy fields guide you to greater pleasures and appreciation of one another. It is dependent on your purpose.

We acknowledge that the outcome of this exercise is also dependent on what we call "spirit" and the guidance systems with which you work. From our experience working with sound, we suggest you can never know what is going to happen when you begin using sound as a cocreative frequency-shifting tool to enhance your well-being. We only know it will be beneficial.

Tantric practice with a partner can involve ceremony or ritual, and we are all for that. You can make whatever room in which you are going to do this exercise into a temple. You may light incense. You may invoke your guides, spirits, angels, deities, and blessings. Ritual helps focus and set the field with intent. Andi, in particular, is an expert at doing this type of ritual. Dedicating the experience to some particular purpose such as world peace or invoking a Buddha of compassion is also quite lovely. Setting an intention before you begin is helpful and can deepen your experience.

Once you begin sounding the sacred vowel sounds, however, something phenomenal occurs. It must be experienced to be understood. In some tantric practices, one visualizes the partner as a divine being, the embodiment of an actual deity. In truth, when you reach this new level of consciousness, you are vibrating at a higher frequency.

Each experience is unique. What occurs for one couple at one time may not occur for the same couple at another time. Sound can be psychotropic and mind-altering, but it is also safe because sound will only take individuals to the level of consciousness they are ready to achieve. We believe that each sound experience you have is divinely guided.

It is important now to present a caveat about sound experiences: Don't compare. Not only are we all unique vibratory beings, but no one ever experiences exactly the same thing. Each and every sound experience you have will be unique to you depending on the time and the place.

It is interesting to note, however, that we've received reports from people who have used these exercises and have actually reported similar inner experiences. Sometimes the people were together in the same room. Sometimes they were separated by both time and space, yet shared very similar experiences. This, indeed, may be an indication of the power of sound and, in particular, the power of the tantra of sound. The implications are quite astounding—that there are not only specific sounds and resonant deities associated with those sounds, but that there are also specific and real planes of consciousness that exist and may be experienced.

Nothing Happened

There are always people in our workshops that have a different inner experience from the majority, or some who seemingly experience nothing out of the ordinary. We acknowledge and honor all these experiences. Each sound experience that you have is as real, valid, and spiritually evolving as the next.

Once a student at one of our Healing Sounds workshops, a lovely person who was the director of a famous orchestra, listened as the participants shared their stories of spiritual phenomena. Someone saw the Eye of God; another was lifted out of his body and transported into the celestial realms. (Such experiences are not uncommon at these workshops.) But this orchestral director simply listened, shrugged his shoulders, and said, "Nothing happened!"

Finally, at the end of the second day, we put this man into the center of the group to do an exercise called "Song of the Soul," in which the group chanted this man's name. At the end of the exercise, this fellow immediately opened his eyes, stood up, and said, "Nothing happened! But thank you for the workshop. I have to leave." Then he walked into a nearby broom closet where he remained for the next half-hour while we completed the workshop. After closure, we went to the broom closet and helped him process his experience. We then grounded him, using sound techniques to bring the energy from his upper chakras to his lower chakras, helping him feel more attuned to his physical body. This allowed him to drive home safely.

We tell this story because it is an example of someone who was comparing his experiences to others. For this man, "Nothing happened!" and yet something indeed did happen. He simply was unaware of what was going on, and perhaps he never did find out what "happened." But it is an example of the importance of not comparing or judging your own experiences against those of others.

Something always happens with every person at their own level of consciousness.

We often perceive that the best experiences are those in which we let ourselves be guided by our own spirit. We encourage you to remain focused with your purpose and intent. Stay open and allow yourselves to have the experience that will be for your highest spiritual development, both individually and as a couple.

In the next chapter, we take you on a similar journey with the *bija* mantras. It is both exciting and powerful, and one that you won't want to miss.

⤳ 10 ⤝

Sounding the *Bijas* with a Partner

Tantra of Sound is most concerned with expanding our awareness through sound to enhance intimacy with ourselves and a partner. It has little to do with sex, but a great deal to do with developing a deeper knowing of ourselves through sound. Sitting in sound for 20 minutes can distract even the most dedicated lotharios, shifting and changing their focus and consciousness to another level. Self-created sounds slow down the heart rate, respiration, and brain waves. Your nervous systems lock in synchrony with each other, and you begin to resonate together. You may experience all sorts of phenomena, from telepathy to past-life recall. You may feel drunk, stoned, or blissed out, or seem to merge into one divine being. (Remember, if you don't experience this, don't compare: We're all unique vibratory beings.) You may feel a deep connection between the two of you unlike anything you have ever experienced before. This intimacy comes from a heart connection that has been established through the sound exercises and the chakra resonance.

Building Your Own Temple

We often listen to our "inner wisdom," which can sometimes manifest as spirit guides. At this moment, as we write, one guide in particular, an old Indian tantric master (speaking with a distinct New Delhi accent) is saying, "Give them the tools and the materials—a hammer, wood, and some nails! But do not tell them how to build their house. They must decide that for themselves. Forget the floor plans and blueprints. These will come when they are ready."

Thus, throughout this book, we give you the tools and the material, the frequency and the intent, and the vocalization and the visualization. We suggest the many possible outcomes. With the above example of using a hammer, wood, and nails, we can suggest the metaphor of using the sound tools we're teaching to create a sacred healing place or perhaps a temple of dedication for yourselves. But who knows, you may end up building a boat or an airplane. Or perhaps even a rocket—the sky (and the universe) is the limit.

We ask that you use your imagination during these exercises with a partner. We trust the energy of sound to such a degree that we know sound coupled with intent will take you and your partner to those places that will be of the highest benefit to you and your relationship. As you may recall, we devoted a chapter to exploring your purpose. This was to help open you up and expand your boundaries of consciousness so that the limitations and expectations you may have about who you are and what you can do may be made clearer, and more easily understood.

Tantra of Sound is about expanding self-awareness and enhancing choice through increased intimacy. When you were younger, your idea of freedom of choice might have been to put your hand in the cookie jar and grab as many chocolate chip cookies as might fit in your grasping fingers. But as you grew up, your notion of freedom of choice probably changed. Perhaps now, given the opportunity to reach into the cookie jar, you might only take one cookie. As you eat it, you might also meditate on the calories or the carbohydrates present in that cookie while your taste buds enjoy the sweet chocolate chip sensations. Perhaps now, as you're reading this book, you may be contemplating the positive qualities that you want to embrace within you and in others, as well as the responsibility you have regarding this.

Important qualities to contemplate when developing an intimate relationship, either with yourself or with another person, are compassion, kindness, open and honest communication, trust, self-love, and self-acceptance. As a trained psychotherapist, however, Andi is all too aware of the challenges and difficulties many people have actually incorporating these beautiful and loving qualities. Often as children we experience deep trauma that can adversely affect us as we grow into adulthood. These inner child emotional woundings need to be healed so that we can experience these uplifting and positive qualities.

Healing the Inner Child

The concept of the "wounded inner child" is a mainstay of modern humanistic and transpersonal psychology. The concept is simple: As children, we experience a traumatic situation; the trauma can be so severe that it stays with us, eventually lodging in our unconscious. For example, we might have been stung by a bee when we were three years old, and from then on experience fear whenever we see a bee. As adults, we may even develop a dislike for honey, and who knows, perhaps insects of all kinds incite fear in us. We don't know exactly why we have these feelings because as adults we have no conscious recollection of the trauma.

Not everyone stung by a bee in childhood is going to grow into a bee-fearing adult because of such a seemingly minor incident. In fact, very few might. But if a child is continually stung by bees throughout childhood, the odds grow considerably in favor of him or her having an adverse reaction to bees that manifests in dysfunctional behavior as an adult.

We use the example of being stung by a bee as a simplification. There are, of course, countless experiences that can emotionally wound us as children, abuse on so many levels—physical, emotional, mental, or even spiritual. Since we are a product of every experience that we have ever had, we carry these emotional scars with us in our unconscious as we grow older. Our adult dysfunctional behavior often stems from these inner child woundings.

In order to heal these wounds, we must consciously address the issues. There are, of course, a multitude of different therapies that exist courtesy of groundbreaking psychologists such as Freud, Jung, Reich, Pearls, Rogers, and many more.

Being able to heal these emotional wounds is possible not only through therapy, but also through loving relationships. One of Andi's favorite quotes is from Eric Fromm, the well-known psychologist, who said, "Nature's natural form of therapy is a loving relationship."

Jonathan acknowledges that the most powerful therapy he has ever encountered involves sound. One experience involved using sound to forgive himself, releasing compassion and loving-kindness to his wounded "inner child." This happened first through conscious awareness of a traumatic issue and acknowledgement of the pain he was experiencing. He then used the power of intention, coupled with the power of sound, to release this specific wounding. He concluded this experience by giving nurturing and love to himself, the adult Jonathan.

For Jonathan, it had to do with learning to generate compassion toward himself by first generating compassion toward little Johnny, the wounded child within. He did this with an exercise we described in an earlier chapter, through toning the heart sound *AH* while projecting the intention and energy of loving-kindness and compassion of his heart chakra to his "inner child."

Compassion

We share this information about healing deep wounds because it is time to express the importance of compassion. What is compassion? It may mean something different to each of us: self-love, unconditional love, empathy, nonjudgment, healing to all sentient beings, kindness. There are so many different possible meanings. The French poet Charles Peguy said, "All life comes from tenderness." The importance of compassion is crucial to our healing and in the experiencing of ourselves in the fullness of who we are as humans.

George Lucas gave an interview to a major magazine just before the release of his first "prequel" *Star Wars* film. He was describing the difference between the Light Side (Jedi Knights) and the Dark Side (the Sith). To paraphrase what he said, it was something like: The Jedi work with compassion, the Sith use greed. We were initially astounded by this statement. We had never considered that an antonym for compassion might be greed, but as we thought about it more, we realized that for many people, the concept of compassion is difficult to understand, but people know what greed is.

Greed is taking more "stuff" than you need. It is selfishness, not selflessness. It is acting from fear because why would you want more than you need, unless you are afraid that you don't have enough? When greed is present, people often get hurt because the greedy person will often go to great lengths to get what he wants.

Fear! Many people believe that it is the opposite energy of love, and we agree. From our perspective, fear is what is responsible for most of the ills on this planet—whether it's people building walls to separate themselves from each other; buying weapons to defend themselves or attack someone else; or stockpiling money, necessary materials, or food (as opposed to sharing it during times of great need). We could go on, but we trust you understand.

Fear brings out the wounded children in all of us. Love is the great healer which allows us to give and be of service to each other. From our perspective, it may be the single most important ingredient to be manifested on the planet. It heals our wounded inner children and helps us realize the interconnectedness between all things. Compassion allows unity of consciousness, which allows us to be kind to each other. In one of his talks, His Holiness the Dalai Lama said, "Just be kind to each other." These simple words have stayed with us and have had a profound effect on us.

In certain indigenous beliefs, one does not do an activity without thinking of the repercussions of this activity for seven generations. For example, you don't cut down a tree if you know that tree might be useful to others for many years to come, rather than just providing firewood for you on cold nights. With greed—the opposite of compassion—you certainly do chop down the tree. In fact, you chop down as many trees as you want because your thoughts are not of anyone else but yourself, because you fear being cold and want a warm fire.

If the world could be as one, with all of us realizing our unity as a divine spark of God/Goddess, as opposed to believing we are all individuals only (sometimes teaming up with my "God" versus your "God"), it would change the planet. In Andrew Harvey's book *Sun at Midnight* (Jeremy P. Tarcher, 2002), he quotes Father Bede Griffiths, the late Benedictine monk and mystic, who said, "In a Mozart symphony, the notes are not confused; every single note and every sophisticated shift of harmony is there, separately, but still contained in one moment." We are all truly contained and connected in the web of life.

Let us begin by working together using sound with the intention of generating compassion. We can guarantee that as you open to the energy of self-acceptance, unconditional love, appreciation, kindness, and tenderness, first toward yourself and then toward others, it will affect the way you lead your life. Unquestionably, it will influence the way you conduct yourself in partnership. Realistically, we know that it is easier said than done, but with the new skills you're developing with the use of sound, it is possible.

Some Tips on *Bija* Mantras

As we return to our exercise for this chapter—experiencing the *bija* mantras with a partner—we trust we have stimulated your awareness of the power of compassion and sound. As we begin this exercise of the *bija* mantras, we're going to suggest that you start by sounding with a partner, toning the mantras on a single note, chanting in a monotone, using the same note for each *bija* mantra, and not necessarily even matching each other's pitch. Again, this is a simple, effective exercise that will balance your chakras and those of your partner.

For those of you who are sonically more adventurous, here are some alternative methods of sounding the *bija* mantras with a partner. They are the same methods we presented when suggesting different ways of sounding the vowels:

• Sound the *bija* mantras on a single note, chanting in a monotone, the same note for each *bija* mantra, and not necessarily matching each other's pitch.

• Sound the *bija* mantras with whatever scale or combination of notes you find comfortable.

• Sound the *bija* mantras using the C-major scale going from C to D to E to F to G to A to B.

• Sound the *bija* mantras using a seven-note major scale starting on whatever note you want.

• Sound the *bija* mantras from your deepest note to your highest note.

Please note that "Frequency + Intent = Healing" and "Vocalization + Visualization = Manifestation."

We cannot repeat these formulas enough, as they are so potent. Please remember them. Please also remember to have fun while doing this exercise. In the Bible it says to make a "joyful" sound, so please be as relaxed and comfortable as you can be. It will assist you and your partner in the exercise.

Beginning the Exercise

As always, sit in a comfortable position, with your back straight. Do this in a place where you will not be disturbed. As suggested previously, while there are numerous postures available, sitting face-to-face works nicely. We add one more suggestion: Don't judge yourself or your partner's sound.

As you may recall from chapter 7, we suggested that you elongate the consonant at the beginning of each *bija* mantra. When we chant these seed syllables, at least one third of the sound (sometimes even half of our breath and therefore of the sound) is devoted to creating this first consonant. With *LAM* for example, if it takes eight seconds to sound the entire word, three or four of those seconds are occupied making the *LLLL* sound while the remaining four seconds are equally split between the *AH* and the *MM* sounds. If we were to phonetically write the pronunciation, it would be something like *LLLLLLLL-AAAH-MMMM*.

For this particular exercise, we want you to focus your attention first on the sound and the chakra. Then, after some practice, you can add a color or a visualization if you wish.

Bija Mantras with a Partner Exercise

Please start by taking a few deep breaths, releasing with a sigh anything that you don't need. Now, as you begin to feel yourself becoming centered, take a moment to focus your thoughts and set

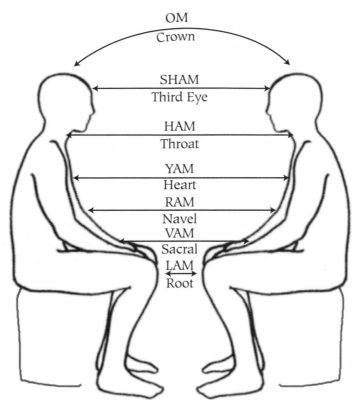

Figure 13 Sounding the *bija* mantras with a partner.

your intention. You may do this silently or out loud, whichever way feels more comfortable.

First *Bija*

We begin with the first (or root) chakra and the mantra *LAM.* Sound the mantra as *LLLLLLL-AAAH-MMM,* using a comfortable pitch. Focus your attention on the root chakra located between your genitals and anus. You may close your eyes while you are making this sound or, better yet, look into your partner's eyes. Feel the sound vibrating this area. Become aware that the energy center associated with this area is also resonating, becoming balanced and aligned. Project this balanced energy from your root chakra into your partner's root chakra, and allow yourself to experience the giving and receiving of the balanced energy from each other's root chakra. Sound the *LAM* mantra together seven times.

Second *Bija*

Now focus your attention on the second (or sacral) chakra, located about three inches below the navel. The *bija* mantra for this is *VAM,* pronounced *VVVVVV-AAAH-MMMM*. Begin to sound the *VAM* in a comfortable pitch. Now focus your attention on the area of the second chakra and project the sound there. As the sound resonates the second chakra, experience this energy center being balanced and aligned. Project this balanced energy from your sacral chakra into your partner's sacral chakra, allowing yourself to experience the giving and receiving of the balanced energy from each other's sacral chakra. Sound the *VAM* mantra together seven times.

Third *Bija*

The *bija* mantra for the third (or navel) chakra, located around the navel, is *RAM*. Begin to tone a very gentle and soft *RAM,* pronounced *RRRRRRRR-AAAH-MMMM*. Focus your attention on the navel area and project the sound there. As the sound resonates this area, experience this energy center balancing and aligning with the other chakras. Project the balanced energy from your chakra into your partner's chakra, allowing yourself to experience the giving and receiving of the balanced energy from each other's third chakra. Sound the *RAM* mantra together seven times.

Fourth *Bija*

The *bija* mantra for the fourth (or heart) chakra, located in the center of your chest, is *YAM*. As previously mentioned, we find it easiest to add an *EEE* sound before the Y to elongate the Y, so that the pronunciation is *EEEEEE-YAAH-MMMM*. Begin to tone this in the same comfortable manner that you have been using. Focus your attention on the heart chakra and project the sound there. As you resonate the heart center with sound, experience this energy center balancing and aligning with the other chakras. Project the balanced energy from your heart chakra into your partner's heart chakra, allowing yourself to experience the giving and receiving of the balanced energy from each other's heart chakra. Sound the *YAM* mantra together seven times.

Fifth *Bija*

Now focus your attention on your fifth (or throat) chakra, located at the throat. The bija mantra for this chakra is *HAM*. (As we mentioned in the chapter on chanting the bija mantras individually, we've found that it's sometimes difficult to make an elongated H sound unless it is an aspirate H that is sounded very softly so that the *HHH* almost rides at first on the breath and then becomes louder.) It's pronounced *HHHHHHH-AAAH-MMMM*. Begin to tone the *HAM* mantra and focus your attention on the throat chakra, projecting sound there. As the sound resonates the throat chakra, experience this energy center balancing and aligning with the other chakras. Project the balanced energy from your throat chakra into your partner's throat chakra, allowing yourself to experience the giving and receiving of the balanced energy from each other's fifth chakra. Sound the *HAM* mantra together seven times.

Sixth *Bija*

Now focus your attention on the sixth chakra, often called the third eye, located on the forehead midway between the eyes and slightly above. The *bija* mantra for this chakra is *SHAM,* pronounced *SSSSHHH-AAAH-MMMM.* Begin to tone that same comfortable note you have been using throughout this exercise. If possible, look into your partner's eyes when making this sound. Now focus your attention on this chakra and project the sound to that area. As the sound resonates the third eye, experience this energy center aligning and balancing with your other chakras. Project the balanced energy from your third eye into your partner's third eye, allowing yourself to experience the giving and receiving of the balanced energy from each other's third eye. Make this *SHAM* sound together seven times.

Seventh *Bija*

The *bija* mantra for the seventh (or crown) chakra, located at the top of the head, is *OM*. For use in this exercise, we simply pronounce it *OOOOOHHH-MMMM*. Begin to tone the *OM* mantra in a comfortable voice. If possible, look into your partner's eyes. Focus your attention on your crown center and begin to project sound there. As the sound resonates the crown chakra, experience this energy center balancing and aligning with the other chakras. Project the balanced energy from your crown chakra into your partner's crown chakra, allowing yourself to experience the giving and receiving of the balanced energy from each other's crown chakra. Chant the *OM* sound together seven times.

Now be in silence.

After 20 minutes of sounding, you and your partner may be light-headed and vibrationally attuned. Sit in this joyful, blissful state of meditation and enjoy this experience.

You have been sounding, resonating, and balancing your chakras as the energy has moved up your spine into your head and above. Allow yourself at least ten minutes for this meditation, and then for however much time as you'd like, stay in silence to have that experience or activity that is for your highest purpose at this particular moment in your mutual development. Allow yourself enough time to enjoy fully the benefits that accompany this toning practice.

Part IV

Other Applications

⌒ 11 ⌒

Toning during Emotional Turmoil

Thus far our center of attention has been on using sound exercises such as Vowels as Mantras and the *Bija* Mantras to resonate ourselves and our partner in order to enhance intimacy in whatever form that may take. In part 4, we'll offer more suggestions for using self-created sound, including alternative sounds to assist in healing relationships that may be experiencing difficulty.

Sometimes a seemingly small thing can trigger an emotional upheaval. It can be helpful to have tools to assist you in moving through the turmoil, particularly when you and your partner are in disharmony and the easiest thing is for one of you to throw a dish, raise your voice, or storm out of the house.

Entrainment 101

Before we talk about these sound strategies that can benefit and help alter your disharmonious relationship moments, we'd like to remind you about entrainment, that phenomenon of sound discussed in chapter 2. Entrainment is the ability of sound to shift and change the vibrational level of a person or persons. On a scientific level, it has to do with psychoacoustics, how sound affects the nervous system and brain.

Entrainment is an aspect of sound closely related to rhythmic sounds and the way these rhythms affect us. It is a phenomenon of sound in which the powerful rhythmic vibrations of one object will cause the less powerful vibrations of another object to lock in step and oscillate at the first object's rate.

The oscillators of television sets, radio receivers, and other similar equipment lock on to each other and entrain. By changing channels on a television, you are adjusting the frequency of your set's oscillators to match the frequency of the broadcast station's oscillators. When the frequencies come close to one another, they suddenly lock, as if they "want" to pulse together. Usually, the fastest oscillator will force the slower ones to operate at its pace.

Like television sets, living organisms such as human beings also oscillate—they pulse, vibrate, and have rhythm. These rhythms of life allow for entrainment. Entrainment is found throughout nature and particularly with human beings. Female college roommates, for example, often have menstrual cycles that synchronize. Muscle cells from the heart, when they move closer together, suddenly shift in their rhythm and start pulsing together, perfectly synchronized. This entrainment also takes place when two people have a good conversation. Their brain waves oscillate synchronously. Such entrainment is seen in the relationship between students and their professors. Psychotherapists and clients entrain with each other, as do preachers and their congregation. Their heart rates, respiration, and brain waves all synchronize with each other due to this phenomenon.

Within our own bodies, we are constantly locking in our own rhythms. Our heart rate, respiration, and brain waves all entrain to each other. If you slow down your breath, for example, you slow down your heartbeat and brain waves. Conversely, if you are able to slow down your brain waves, you can affect your heart rate and respiration. This is one of the principles of biofeedback. Just as the functions of the human body can entrain to each other, it is possible to use external rhythms to affect the internal mechanisms of heart rate, respiration, and brain wave activity.

Through working with self-created sounds with someone else, this often occurs mutually, allowing us to resonate with each other—shifting and changing the rhythms of our brain waves, heartbeat, and respiration. It is not necessary for either partner to be in a state of bliss and surrender when initially working with self-created sounds in order to create harmony between them. Self-created sounds can shift the frequency levels of both people simultaneously. This is huge because frequently during times of disharmony in a relationship our natural response is the fight-or-flight mechanism: We're either going head-on with our partner or we're leaving.

Fight or Flight versus Frequency Shifting

What if it were possible to offer a third alternative to disharmony? Instead of fight or flight, what if we considered frequency shifting through the focused use of self-created sound as a reaction to disharmony?

We know how difficult this can be. Too often, when we've reached disharmony (anger, sadness, fear—whatever it may be), it's so much easier for us to react with hastily chosen words or behaviors that unconsciously come from our emotional wounding. What you'll begin to notice is that even this is an aspect of entrainment. Yes, the phenomenon of entrainment is not only useful for creating harmony and peace between partners, it's also often responsible for *creating* disharmony.

Have you ever been in a situation where you were feeling calm and relaxed, and then your partner charged into the room with some irritating problem he was having? Despite your seeming calmness, within moments you might both be shouting. This is entrainment. Remember, entrainment goes both ways: It can be used to create harmony, but the phenomenon of frequency has no conscience and can also create disharmony. Thus, if you're in a meeting and the leader wants to get everyone charged up, all she has to do is a little shouting with some well-chosen words and, suddenly, a previously calm environment can become one of hysteria and anger. This too is entrainment. Sometimes the larger the group, the easier it is for the leader to change the frequency level of the group through well-chosen sounds.

With regard to relationships, we ask again: What if, instead of being reactive and either fighting or fleeing during times of disharmony, one of the people in the relationship had the awareness to use sound to drown the fires of the fight-or-flight mechanism?

On one level, this seems unrealistic, but what if we told you it could actually work and be effective? Emotional reactions, particularly in times of stress, are difficult to handle, but we have some basic sound strategies that are easy to implement.

The Scenario of John and Mary

John and Mary have been living together for a while. They deeply love each other and, of course, there are issues that they need to heal. They may not have yet dealt with their wounded inner child. It's dinnertime. John has returned from a hard day at the office and he's hungry. Mary's had her own difficult day and the dinner she promised to put on the table is not yet cooked. John has said something to Mary about her promising to take care of dinner that night. Perhaps she has misinterpreted what John has said, or perhaps he's inadvertently being cruel. Either way, her words begin to heat up and then so do his.

Things escalate and Mary has now delivered a verbal *coup de grace* to John, pushing all of his emotional buttons. He does the same to her. Now, John is raging. So is Mary. Something has to give.

We know that just as there are repeating patterns caused by our unconscious inner-child wounds, there are arguments that continually occur between couples usually over similar, if not exactly the same, repeated issues.

We have been in similar situations. Everyone has. One of the greatest temporary healing mechanisms we want to share with you is simply to make a sound together. Yes, that's all there is to it. Stop your shouting; put down the plate; stop packing for your mother's; put down your overcoat and don't walk out the door! Instead, take a breath, look each other in the eyes, and sound an *AH* or an *OM* three times together. It can be challenging, but if you can do it, the energy between you two will shift. It takes practice, but it is well worth it in the long run. It can create an opening for you to get back to the love that has temporarily been misplaced. It can shift the actual frequency of the moment and open up a space for you to communicate with each other in a sane manner.

As we've mentioned previously, the simple *AH* sound is a great one to make to activate compassion and heart energy. So is *OM*. If both partners can momentarily cease their arguing and sound together for just a few moments, the results can be astounding. Sounding together like this can generate empathy and loving-kindness between the two of you as you both experience frequency shifts.

This may sound unfathomable for couples locked in the throes of a heated argument, but we must tell you how effective this exercise is. Give it a try!

Through entrainment on a physiological level, you will both immediately begin to calm your heart rate, brain waves, and respiration. After even only that first breath followed by an *AH* or *OM* sound, you will start to experience immediate transformation on an emotional or mental level.

We guarantee that if you try making a sound together in the midst of a fight, you will feel different. The only difficulty, of course, is remembering to do it. Discussing this particular strategy ahead of time when you're both in a positive state is helpful. Give yourselves permission to practice, and set the intention that you'll do your best when the heated battle happens.

Make an Agreement to Sound

If both partners agree that the next time they are in a disharmonious situation, one will suggest they make a sound together, or perhaps just start making a sound, this will work well. A tool to help is for one person in the relationship to say something like, "Hold on for a minute. Would you make a sound with me?" Often having a key word or phrase agreed on ahead of time can be beneficial when you find yourself in a disharmonious situation that you want to change. Jonathan likes to say "Quick— make an Om!" Andi says: "Please Om with me, now!"

Again, we know how difficult it is to shift the psychological patterns and loops we're usually caught in at these times. It takes almost a superhuman (or should we say superconscious) effort on the part of one of the people to even break away from the loop for a moment to suggest this alternative. But if the other person can just nod his head and for a moment agree to sound (with all his anger and fury intact), they might find relief.

It is one thing to be sitting in a beautifully decorated room with candles burning and beautiful colored lights glowing while you sound the sacred vowels or the *bija* mantras together in order to initiate a tantric experience between the two of you. It is quite another to be snarling at each other and be able to take a few moments to create healing sounds. Perhaps when you and your partner are sitting in your beautifully decorated "tantric temple" sounding together, you can use this as a time to agree to tone together at some later time of disharmony, thereby re-creating a harmonious relationship with each other.

In other words, make an agreement ahead of time so when you do find yourself in a battle situation, you'll make an effort to sound together before either of you does one of your more drastic routines (walking out the door, dropping dishes). As a suggestion, we can think of no better time or situation to make this agreement than when you are both in harmony with each other after having just resonated your chakras together in sound.

The John and Mary Scenario—Revisited

John and Mary have just completed one of the two powerful sonic exercises we've presented. Whether they've used the *bija* mantras or the sacred vowels, they are in harmony. Their nervous systems, heart rate, respiration, and brain waves—not to mention their chakras and etheric fields—are in resonance with each other. They look at each other adoringly and see the god and goddess within. They are both divine entities who have manifested on the physical level to enjoy all its wondrous sensations. As they gaze lovingly into each other's eyes, they realize how powerful sound is as a tool to create harmony within themselves and between them.

At this magic tantric moment, John says to Mary (or perhaps vice versa): "Honey, if we ever find ourselves arguing, let's remember to use sound to get ourselves back in balance." And Mary agrees. At that time, they have programmed themselves (and their higher consciousness) to do that most difficult of tasks: toning during emotional turmoil. At some later time, this agreement will allow one of these partners during the height of battle to say the words: "Let's stop and make sound!" With this, the power of sound can start shifting and changing their reality.

(Now, of course, we know that after you and your partner have been engaged in these magic tantric moments as have just been described, you will never again be out of harmony or resonance with each other—and thus the need for toning during trauma will not be necessary! But, just in case it is, you'll be ready!)

Toning during Stress

Toning during emotional stress is excellent if you're feeling out of harmony with your partner, but it's also beneficial if you're feeling out of harmony with yourself. It can be done at any time—you don't have to be in the fumes of a fight. You can simply be at the place where the jagged edge of discomfort has begun to emerge. When that happens, stop, take a deep breath, and get some *OM*s or *AH*s out as soon as possible.

Odds are the jagged edge will disappear and you'll soon be in a harmonious state to discuss and heal whatever is bothering you. Usually, we find when making sounds during turbulent emotional moments that whatever the initial instigator of the problem might have been—late dinner, early breakfast, whatever—it will eventually seem insignificant. You might even end up laughing about the silliness of the whole thing.

When you make sounds in the heat of an argument, odds are that even if your tones together in the tantric temple were sweet and angelic, in the midst of a fight, you'll be lucky if either of your sounds are more than a grunt. That first *AH* or *OM* can be difficult to sound and, usually, it's not going to be harmonious. But remember, it is frequency plus intent. Even if you're only halfheartedly agreeing to make a sound together, once those gruntlike tones begin to emerge, the results can be surprising.

Here's another hint: If you find that making three tones of *AH* or *OM* isn't enough, go for more. In difficult situations, making even more sound is recommended as necessary for restoring balance. Sometimes it takes a few minutes of sound to put you back in resonance with each other. Usually, making those first three tones is enough to put each of you into an emotional place where you realize the need for creating more sound together. Taking time to restore harmony is probably a lot better than one of you spending a sleepless night on the sofa. Sometimes, as stated, it only takes three simple *AH* sounds—particularly effective when sounded with compassion from the heart—to change the outcome. Whatever it takes, it's worth it.

This chapter would not be complete if we did not bring in and honor the work of our dear friend and master sound healer Sarah "Saruah" Benson, an extraordinary teacher of sound and love who has shared many different powerful sound exercises with us. Those of you who have read *Healing Sounds* know that Sarah was Jonathan's original initiator into the mysteries of sound; Sarah later became one of Andi's important teachers of sound as well. One of Sarah's main areas of expertise is working with sound to heal the emotional body.

Sarah has a seemingly endless vocabulary of emotional sound healing techniques. For this book, we offer one of our favorites, an exercise we call the "Lullaby to Your Inner Child." Those of you who are parents know the power of a lullaby when your little loved one can't sleep or is in pain and needs soothing and nurturing. With a lullaby, you naturally do this with sound. Here is an exercise in which you can do self-healing for own your inner child, soothing and nurturing yourself through your own self-created sound.

Lullaby to Your Inner Child

A lullaby to your own inner child is a remarkable sonic tool useful for healing the wounded child within. It's simple and easy. First, find yourself a comfortable space where you will not be disturbed by anyone. Next, set forth an intention of unconditional love and tenderness toward your precious inner child. It's important to create a space where you will have the freedom to make sound without needing to be conscious of your voice. It's important that you have this freedom with all of the exercises in this book, but particularly with this one. You probably won't be very loud at all, but it's nice to have that option for whatever sounds need to manifest for this exercise.

Begin by hugging yourself and imagining yourself getting in touch with your inner child. You may want to hold a pillow or a stuffed animal with your eyes closed as you're bringing your inner child into your mind's eye. Imagine how old you are and what you look like: Are you an infant or a toddler? What are you wearing? Begin to hum gently for as long as you like. Let the humming slowly and comfortably turn into a lullaby that you sing to yourself. Imagine all the loving thoughts being sung to a precious child. If possible, don't try to sing some preconceived melody, just allow yourself to be a conduit of the sound that wants to come through.

If we've learned anything from Sarah, it is to trust the sound current, that is, to believe in the power of unconscious sound coupled with unconditional love to create miracles. Allow the sound of the lullaby to come through you as you hold and hug the child within. If it wants, the sound will grow from the hum you initially created to a tone with a melody that nourishes your child within. Words may even accompany these sounds. Allow yourself the ability to create whatever sounds want to emerge from you. You may find that within a few minutes of singing this lullaby (it will be glorious, regardless of the tones or tunes you use), your child within will be nurtured by these emotionally healing sounds.

Toning your inner child's lullaby is a wonderful exercise that you must experience to understand. Sound can bypass that part of the brain and psyche where all our barriers and blocks remain, accessing areas of the conscious and unconscious that have been hidden or distant from us. By toning the Lullaby to Your Inner Child, you may be able to comfort and heal an aspect of yourself that has not been accessible before. You may even be able to heal deep issues.

The Lullaby to Your Inner Child is not just for you. You can do it with your partner, particularly in times of difficulty. It requires great amounts of trust and intimacy on both your parts, but the rewards are worth it. When you reach that place where either of you (or perhaps both of you) is willing to receive the power of this exercise, all you do is this: One of you will surrender to the other, lying in the arms of your partner to be comforted and cuddled while you are being sung a special lullaby created just for you at this moment.

While in this state of surrender, your partner will begin to tone the Lullaby to Your Inner Child for you. You may feel uncomfortable at first because this lullaby has such power to reach deep within those hidden parts of you. But as the sound continues you will feel a deep emotional resonance occurring within you. Receive! Receive the love and blessings that are being bestowed on you through the sound.

And if you want, and if it feels appropriate, you may tone along with your partner as well. But we first recommend just receiving the light and love through sound that is being created by the Lullaby to Your Inner Child.

Experiment with these basic strategies for using sound to create shifts and changes during emotional turmoil or stressful situations of any nature. These exercises work. Give them a try. Utilize them with the loving power of intention, and see what a difference that makes in your life and in your relationships.

～ 12 ～

Overtones and Other Sounds

In the previous sections, we have focused primarily on using the tools of the *bija* mantras and the sacred vowel sounds. If these were the only self-created sounds that you were ever to work with, they would be enough for a lifetime, perhaps several lifetimes. We would be remiss, however, if we did not mention four additional sounds that we have worked with and found to be particularly useful for frequency shifting.

The first of these sounds manifested for Jonathan during his research into vocal harmonics as he describes in *Healing Sounds*. It is the *NURR* sound (or as we sound it, *NNNN-UUUU-RRRR*). This sound is used to open a new chakra, called the Angel chakra, located midway between the third eye and crown chakra. (We discuss this chakra later in this chapter.) This sound is great to use individually or with a partner while projecting light into this area.

The second of these sounds, *MUAHZIDT,* was shared with us by our dear friends Jill Schumacher and Meredith McCord, nurse practitioners and healers who have done groundbreaking work in vibration and sound with the ancient Egyptian Mysteries. This sound is part of an ancient Egyptian practice called the "Great Work," in which energy was moved from the root chakra through the crown chakra to balance and align the energy centers and energy bodies. We've added a bit more to the sound than what we had initially received and pronounce it *MMMM-OOOO-AAAAHHH-ZZZ-III-DDD-TTT.*

The third of these sounds, *VIZ,* has an unknown origin. It came to us through a meditation on the Nature kingdom. It is pronounced *VVVV-IIII-ZZZZ.* We explain more about this sound later in the chapter.

The fourth sound is much like the *AH* or *OM* sound. It is a universal sound that many believe to be the name for the Divine. Out of all the sounds in this chapter, this sound is certainly the most known, found in many different traditions. It is the *HU* sound, powerful when sounded individually or with a partner.

The *NURR* Sound

We use the *NURR* sound to teach vocal harmonics. It rhymes with the word "her." It is phonetically written *NNNN-UUUU-RRRR.*

As clear light is actually made of the full spectrum of colors, so sounds that we hear and create are made of a spectrum of tones called harmonics or overtones. Harmonics are sounds within sounds that make up the texture of tone; they are, in fact, the components that create the timbre or tone color of sound.

These harmonics, or overtones, are mathematically related to each other so that the first overtone vibrates twice as fast as the fundamental tone, the second overtone vibrates three times as fast as the fundamental, the third overtone vibrates four times as fast as the fundamental, and so on. Each succeeding overtone goes faster and faster. This does not mean, however, that we can actually differentiate or hear overtones—particularly very high, fast ones. Overtones are no more individually recognizable than the colors of the spectrum in clear light. With light, you can use a prism to separate the colors. With overtones, you can develop ways of using your voice to separate and amplify harmonics. In particular, you can use the vowel sounds as presented in this book. No doubt, as many of you worked with the exercises utilizing vowels, you were puzzled by some mysterious sounds that appeared while you were sounding the vowel. You may have heard a whistling sound, a buzzing sound, or perhaps a ghostlike voice. These are overtones, or harmonics, created by your voice.

Specific overtones are associated with each of the vowel sounds and manifest as they are vocalized. These overtones, created from vowel sounds, are the first ten or so overtones of the overtone series. Some well-trained overtone singers can actually generate many more overtones through specific techniques.

Since this is not a book on overtones, we have not discussed this subject until now because you can do any of the previous exercises in this book easily without any conscious knowledge of overtones. However, with the *NNNN-UUUU-RRRR* sound, it is difficult to describe without bringing overtones into your awareness.

The *NNNN-UUUU-RRRR* sound was originally taught to Jonathan back in the mid-1980s by Dr. Ted Levin, a member of the Harmonic Choir, as a sound that would enhance the creation of vocal overtones. There are many different techniques for doing this; the use of vowel sounds is merely one. When creating this sound, Jonathan was told to first get his nose vibrating with a *NNNN* sound. Besides being an essential part of creating vocal harmonics, this *NNNN* sound, incidentally, can help open your sinus passageways if you have a cold.

Try this *NNNN* sound, getting your nose to vibrate. Many people find it best to add an *EEEE,* so it sounds like an elongated version of the word "knee." It's helpful to put a finger on either side of your nose in order to feel the sensations of your nasal cavity vibrating. We've found that people occasionally have difficulty bringing the sound up into their head and making this nasal sound; instead, the *NNNN* sound vibrates mostly down in their chest. In these circumstances, we have our students pretend they're children, going "Nah-Nah-Nah-Nah-Nah." All of a sudden, the sound is up in their head, and they're able to feel the resonance of the *NNNN* sound.

The next part of the *NNNN-UUUU-RRRR* sound involves making the *UUUU* sound. This *UUUU* sound is made in the back of the throat; it's very guttural, as though you were making the *UH* sound, the vowel sound of the first chakra.

Now bring the sound to the front of your mouth with the *RRRR* sound. Some people find it easy to make this sound; it's a sound from childhood like when we made the sound of an engine or a plane taking off. With the *RRRR* sound, your tongue is about a quarter-inch to a half-inch behind your teeth; it is not touching the roof of your mouth, but vibrating on a layer of saliva. Some people also curve their tongues for this. If you are having difficulty, try adding an *EEEE* to this, so that you are making the elongated sound *RRRREEEE* (as in "he").

You're probably getting your nose vibrating with the *NNNNN* sound, bringing it to the back of the throat with the *UUUUU* sound, and bringing the sound forward with the *RRRR* sound. (Another way that you can try this sound is by adding an *EEEE* sound at the end and pronouncing it, *NNNNEEEE-UUUU-RRRREEEE*.) If you have made the sound in these three different places, you should be hearing a high, whistlelike sound. These are audible overtones you have created from the *NURR* sound. As you experiment with the *NURR* sound, continue being nasal as you make the sound and slightly move your tongue around the roof of your mouth when you come to the *RRRR* part. Adding the *EEEE* sound at the end may be particularly helpful in hearing higher harmonics.

The *NURR* Sound and Light

There are a number of interesting aspects to the *NURR* sound. It is excellent for learning to create vocal harmonics. It is a word for "light" in a number of mid-eastern and Eastern languages. *NURR* is the sound that Jonathan made in a Mayan temple in Palenque that caused the chamber to become illuminated. Here is what happened.

Jonathan was in Mexico in 1987 for the Harmonic Convergence. One evening, he was in a Mayan temple with a group of people. The guide, who must have had esoteric knowledge, pointed to a doorway in the temple and said to Jonathan, "Make sound here," then he turned off his flashlight. Jonathan made the *NURR* sound. The room became illuminated. More than a half-dozen people experienced this. The guide then turned his flashlight back on. There was no discussion and the group moved on, but the experience never left Jonathan.

The Angel Chakra

Ten years later, we were teaching the *NURR* sound in a workshop, and Jonathan became aware that a powerful energy was being projected from the skulls of the students. He realized that the energy was being projected in the area between the third eye and crown. This area, which we call the Angel chakra, seems to be associated with the inpouring and outpouring of light into and from the body.

In our workshops, we now have students make this *NURR* sound while visualizing the sound going through the roof of the mouth, up through the sinus cavity and into the pituitary-pineal-hypothalamus area, causing light to be projected out from (and at the same time, received into) this area. It is one of the most powerful initiations people have experienced in our workshops.

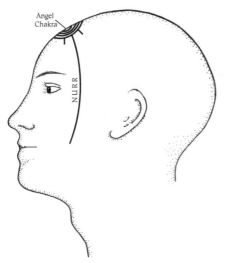

Figure 14 The location of the Angel chakra and the path of the NURR Sound to activate it.

We have given elaborate explanations of the *NURR* sound so you will be able to experience it easily. It is nice to do by yourself, and even better to experience with a partner. This sound exercise is a wonderful way to share light and love by connecting your Angel chakras.

The Angel chakra appears to be a new chakra that is becoming activated now for many people who are working with higher consciousness. It seems to be a way of bringing more light and higher vibrations into the physical and etheric bodies from higher dimensions. It is also a way of getting information from guides and angelic beings, thus the name Angel chakra.

We recommend that you activate and utilize the Angel chakra after you have activated all seven chakras through the sound exercises in this book. In addition, we suggest that this activation of the Angel chakra should occur separately and at another time than working with the seven major chakras.

The Angel chakra's midway location between the third eye and crown suggests that it possesses qualities that are a little more spiritual than the third eye, and a little less transpersonal than the crown chakra. It is an exciting new area for those who are doing advanced work with energy and relationships.

We've had fun teaching people to hug each other while making an *AH* sound and projecting the energy of love to each other, or to put their skulls together and make an *OM* sound. Both of these exercises are exhilarating, but working with the *NURR* sound is different. Perhaps because of its power and its effectiveness, we suggest caution when choosing a partner. It accesses intimacy unlike anything we've encountered before.

A Tantric Exercise for *NURR*

Put your heads together so your foreheads touch about three inches above the eyebrow line. Make the *NURR* sound together and visualize celestial light pouring in, meeting and blending with your partner's celestial light. As you make this sound, feel your own light going into your partner's Angel chakra, and at the same time receive the light from your partner. It's a wonderful exercise after you've completed any act of intimacy, including, of course, lovemaking. Putting your heads together and chanting *NURR* in this manner provides a deep sharing of energies. We recommend that you use discernment in choosing the person with whom you do this exercise. We have not suggested such constraint before, but with this particular sound, we do.

Note that while this exercise is a great way to blend your energies after you have done Vowels as Mantras or *Bija* Mantras, we suggest you allow some time between these exercises. Often less sound is better and more effective; too much sound can deplete the effect of the sound. You can overload on sound, to the degree where the power of the sound becomes nullified. Since we want you to have the best experience possible, we make this suggestion.

In workshops where we have many people undergoing transformational experiences with sound, we have breaks between the exercises. These allow the sounds to be assimilated and enable activation of new sounds. Remember the importance of silence. Whether you're working with yourself or a partner, do not overdo it out of enthusiasm. Sufficient time between the sound exercises will enhance the effect of the sonic experiences.

MUAHZIDT

MUAHZIDT (MMMM-OOOO-AAAAHHH-ZZZ-III-DDD-TTT) seems to be a fast way of moving energy through all the chakras, from the root to crown. This apparently was one of its uses in ancient Egypt— as a sound to bring energy through the body and align the subtle bodies. It is useful after the chakras have been aligned and one has experienced the ultimate harmonization of lovemaking. It is a wonderful sound to experiment with by putting your heads together, making this sound, and then directing the energy into one each other.

With *MUAHZIDT,* the *MMMMM* creates the sound that seems to resonate the skull as well as the crown chakra. Then, with intention, bring this energy down to the first chakra with the *UUU* (or use the

OOO sound if it's easier). Next, bring the energy up to the heart center with the *AH* sound. The *ZZZZ* sound brings the energy up to the pituitary/pineal area. With the *DDD-TTT* sound, the energy is then expelled out of the head. This energy can be projected from the third eye, Angel chakra, or crown chakra into the same chakra of your partner.

As noted, the origin of this mantra is an ancient Egyptian practice called the "Great Work," which brings the energy up from the root to the crown chakra to commune with the Divine. This energy travels up the spinal column and is the life energy called kundalini. It is said to be a coiled serpent that sleeps in the root chakra; upon awakening, it rises up the spine, eventually reaching the head.

The raising of kundalini is considered by swamis and yogis to be a powerful and important aspect of spiritual evolution. As the chakras resonate and open, the kundalini rises. Various sensory experiences are enhanced, resulting in heightened comprehension, intuition, and visualization. Eventually, different powers and abilities, called *siddhis,* begin to manifest. These *siddhis* can include teleportation, mind-reading, and even weather control. Ultimately, when the kundalini has made its way up the crown chakra, divine consciousness is opened. The *MUAHZIDT* sound, in particular, was used in this manner as a tool to bring this energy up through the chakras for spiritual activation and to balance and align the different subtle bodies.

We have not had much experience working with this mantra on an individual basis, but we have had success working together as a couple with this sound. *MUAHZIDT* allows us to actively propel energy up and out of our bodies into each other's head chakras. It is powerful sound that rapidly moves energy, and we have had wonderful experiences with it.

The Difference between *NURR* and *MUAHZIDT*

What is the difference between *NURR* and the *MUAHZIDT*? As we are all unique vibratory beings, we can only suggest that you experiment with these sounds and see how they resonate with you.

In our experience, *NURR* is the sound we use for the activation of the Angel chakra to bring more light and love into our physical and etheric bodies. People have all sorts of powerful experiences with this sound. When the sound is successfully activated, people frequently talk about a shaft of spiraling light that comes down through their head into the heart center, and then spreads throughout their body. This is one of the more frequently described experiences, but we have heard dozens of other experiences. There are many possibilities of what can happen, including nothing (please remember the "nothing happened" story). It's a splendid sound that we happily share with you.

In the Egyptian "Great Work," the sound *MUAHZIDT* was used to bring energy from the root chakra to the crown chakra, much as we have been doing with Vowels as Mantras and the *Bija* Mantras. The *U* or *OOO* sound resonates the lower chakras, the *AH* resonates the heart chakra, and the *ZIDT* focuses on the *EEE* sound to bring the energy to the chakras of the head.

Both the *NURR* and *MUAHZIDT* sounds are different and powerful. After you have worked with each, you will understand their different functions and purposes in your own life.

VIZ

We discovered the *VIZ* sound one day while meditating with the nature kingdom. We found it to be a powerful sound that resonates the energy at the back of the head, in the area slightly above where the neck and the skull meet. By sounding the *VIZ*, energy can be brought from this region at the back of head up through the skull to the forehead. While sounding the *VIZ*, we can feel a stream of energy being projected outward from the forehead, around the third eye area—the sixth chakra.

The back of the head is often associated with the primitive brain. This part of the brain is nonrational and involved with aspects of survival. It is constantly scanning for experiences that induce the fight or flight response in order to protect us. However, it can also hold old patterns of trauma that can be triggered, keeping us from experiencing the reality of the present moment. Sometimes a particular behavior, person, or sensation will trigger a past trauma that can activate an old emotional wound within us. This could be something that may not be relevant to the present situation, but nevertheless grips us in its power. We may experience, for example, trauma such as panic for no apparent reason. The *VIZ* sound has the potential to transform such energies of past traumas into more harmonious patterns congruent with what is currently happening.

A *VIZ* Exercise

Close your eyes and begin sounding a very gentle *VVVVV* sound, focusing your attention on the back of your head at the indentation a little above where the spinal column meets the skull (see figure 15). Close your mouths slightly so that your lips are gently vibrating with this sound. Consciously project this *VVVVV* sound to the back of your head. As you feel the sound vibrating there, slowly begin to change the sound to an *IIIIII* (sounding like an *EH* which is between the vowels *AYE* and *EEE*). You may feel the sound somewhere in the middle of your head. Then change the sound again, to a *ZZZZ* sound. To make the *ZZZZZ* sound, your tongue

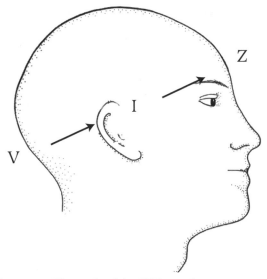

Figure 15 The path of the *VIZ* sound.

moves forward and touches the roof of your mouth, bringing the sound to the sinus area and above. Visualize the sound traveling into your forehead. Feel the vibrations moving to your third eye. Continue visualizing this energy moving from the back of your head to your forehead, around your third eye. Notice what you're feeling.

Now try this exercise while focusing on an old pattern of behavior that is no longer appropriate—some irrational fear, emotion, or belief that no longer serves you. Sound the *VIZ* and focus your intention on the sound moving from the back of your head up to your forehead, releasing it out your third eye. Make this sound and visualization three times. Many times, simply sounding the *VIZ*, coupled with the visualization of releasing the outmoded behavior, can transform it through the energies of the higher brain functions associated with the frontal lobe area around the third eye. It can produce extremely powerful and beneficial effects. You may find the *VIZ* to be one of the most powerful and harmonious sounds for healing the wounded "inner child," and excellent for transmuting trauma.

Trust Your Inner Wisdom

As always, fluidity is key in creating sacred sound. While you may have a desired outcome and intent with the sound, ultimately the sound will do what it wants—it will take you where it needs to go. It may not be what you expected, but it will bring you whatever is for your highest good and growth at that particular moment.

Here is a story of what happened to Jonathan before he met Andi, when he was conducting a workshop using sound and crystals. In a meditation, participants were led through a visualization using sound and crystals, and then left to meditate. At the end of the experience, a woman had a scowl on her face. Jonathan asked about her experience.

"Well," the woman began, "you said we could go wherever we wanted, so I decided to go and meet my spirit guide. There I was in this beautiful field, with all these lovely flowers and trees and all of a sudden, this dirty old Indian runs by. He's half naked, wearing a loin cloth, and turns to look at me, beckoning me to follow him. Well, I'm waiting for my spirit guide, so naturally I just ignore him. It was really disappointing. My spirit guide never showed up."

Jonathan's heart went out to this disappointed participant, and he gently suggested that perhaps "the dirty old Indian" was indeed her spirit guide, perhaps a powerful shaman who wanted to teach her some powerful medicine.

"No," this woman argued, "my spirit guide would have been dressed all in white, like a holy man. He would have to be."

We share this story because it shows how we may have expectations about spiritual experiences, but in reality what we are expecting and what we need and get may be entirely different.

Tantra of Sound focuses on personal empowerment, allowing individuals to grow without limiting their experiences by putting boundaries on them. We encourage each of you to trust your experiences, to trust your inner guidance as you explore the exercises.

HU, the Sound of Creation

Let's now examine the *HU* sound. Just as many traditions believe that the *OM* is the original creative sound, and other traditions believe that the *AH* is the original creative sound, so there are traditions that believe that the *HU* is the fundamental sound energy. In the Shabd yoga traditions of India, as well as the Westernized counterpart of Shabd yoga (Master Path and Eckankar), and in the mystical Islamic path of Sufi, *HU* is considered to be the highest vibratory mantra that can be sounded. Chanting the *HU* is said to lead one to transcendence, God realization, and enlightenment.

HU is believed to be the universal name of God, present in every language. The *HU* sound has been described as many things: the buzzing of bees, rushing of wind, the flute of God. It is said to be present in the words we speak, in the sounds of animals, the wind in the trees, the roaring of waterfalls, or the beat of the sea against a beach—everywhere, in every plane of existence.

Like the *AH* and the *OM*, the *HU* is a seed syllable. Depending on its pronunciation, it may also be perceived as a vowel sound, the U (as in "you"). The *HU* creates energy for balance and clearing. Many believe it activates both heart and crown chakras. When sounded together in a large group, it can be extremely transformative.

Not surprisingly, different spiritual paths seem to have different ways of pronouncing the *HU*, the sacred name of God. Certain spiritual paths from the Shabd yoga traditions chant it as "you." Other variants of Shabd yoga chant it as "who." In the Sufi tradition, there is even a special way of chanting the *HU:* lips barely touching, this being the primary vibrator of the sound so that this *HU* sounds almost like a motorboat or a buzzing insect.

Different groups may insist that their pronunciation of *HU* is the only correct pronunciation, but regardless of the way it is chanted, continued elongated sounding of *HU* with intent and visualization can lead one into elevated consciousness.

Combining Sounds

In this chapter we have presented four sounds that can be used for personal and partnered transformation. These are sounds we have worked with individually and with groups, and found effective. We have presented them here for your personal enjoyment and transformation. There are hundreds, perhaps thousands, of other sounds that may also generate vibrational experiences for you.

Just as there are many culinary dishes to be sampled, we are never averse to trying combinations of sounds from different cultures. Sometimes combining sounds creates mantras. For example, if you take the *AH*, the *HU*, and the *OM* and put them together, you basically have the great cleansing chant from the Tibetan Buddhist tradition: *OM AH HUM*.

In Tibetan Buddhism, *OM AH HUM*, the Mantra of Blessing, frequently precedes the recitation of other mantras. In the context of this mantra, *OM* represents the principle of the universal body resonating the crown center; the *AH* embodies the principle of creative sound and pure speech that resonates the throat chakra; and the *HUM* is the principle of the love of the enlightened mind of all Buddhas in the heart center. This mantra is used at the beginning of many rituals and blessings because of its power to purify negativity and amplify positive energy.

Another example is to combine a vowel from Vowels as Mantras and a *bija* from the *Bija* Mantras. For instance, when resonating the second chakra, you combine the vowel and the *bija* from the second chakra and come up with the sound *OOO-VAM*. Or, for the heart, you'd use the vowel and the *bija* for the fourth chakra and come up with *AH-YAM*. You get the idea. You could also reverse the position with the *bija* coming first, so for the heart chakra it would be *YAM-AH*. The possibilities are endless.

We stress the importance of allowing time between the different sound exercises. For example, going directly from Vowels as Mantras to *Bija* Mantras may be too much. Sonic overload can seemingly occur in situations where the silence between the sounds is not honored. When this happens, the vitality of the exercise is diminished. Give yourself time between the different sound experiences.

Sometimes other mantras and other sacred sounds will come to us from people, books, recordings, in meditation, or in dreams. Usually, our only prerequisite for trying a new mantra is to have some knowledge of its purpose. Since we understand our uniqueness as vibratory beings, we know that we may not have the same experiences. As journeyers on the path of sound, however, we do want some sense of what the sound is supposed to do. If it's "Frequency + Intent," then we have to take responsibility in terms of our knowledge of sacred sound.

Nearly 25 years ago, at the start of his journey with sound, Jonathan attended a group with devotees of a guru. There were about 30 people in the room, and after a welcoming talk by the director of this group, a piece of paper was handed to everyone, and the people in the room were told they were going to chant. Jonathan looked at the paper and realized that the chant was in a language he didn't understand. In his naiveté (or perhaps his wisdom), he asked what the chant meant and what it was used for. No one in the room, including the person directing the session, had a clue, but since it came from their guru they had no doubt that it was good. Jonathan asked how they could possibly be chanting something if they didn't know what it meant, or what it was for. He was politely asked to leave.

From our perspective, we believe that if you are going to chant sacred sounds from another language, it's important to have some idea about what you're chanting. There are thousands of different and specific chants, and usually many of them are effective. This is wonderful, but if you don't want to chant for rain on the third Tuesday of the month, or for a big dinner of beans and rice or whatever, then you shouldn't do so. You have the right to know the meaning of a particular chant. Be aware and trust your inner guidance.

Explore the sacred sounds from the myriad different traditions on the planet. If you encounter a mantra (a sacred phrase) that resonates with you, we encourage you to begin practicing with it. There are Sanskrit mantras. Hebrew mantras. Tibetan mantras. Native American mantras. Islamic mantras. Swahili mantras. Japanese mantras. Latin mantras. Greek mantras. Aramaic mantras. Inuit mantras. Mayan mantras. Chinese mantras. English mantras. We could go on and on, but you get the idea.

Be discriminating with the sounds you make. Know on outer and inner levels that the sacred sound you are about to make is right for you. It's doubtful that you could damage yourself or do injury, but it's important to know what the mantra means, where it came from, how it is supposed to be used, and what its particular effect might be. If possible, once you feel a resonance with a mantra or sound, stick with it for a while. Perseverance is important. With the exercises in this book, the more you focus on one exercise the better you will be at doing it, and the more effective it will be. Don't be a sonic butterfly, flitting from one sound bite to the next, sampling the vibrations of mantras from different traditions but never embracing any one sound.

Now, here's one last story thanks to Dr. Randall McClellan, a pioneer in the field of sound and healing, who first shared it many years ago.

Abdul and the Extraordinary Instrument

Abdul had an extraordinary instrument, beautifully carved with many long strings. He would play this wondrous instrument for hours every day. But unlike his friends who would play glorious melodies and harmonies on their instruments, Abdul just plucked one string over and over for hours. One day, his dear wife could no longer take it and said, "Oh, dear husband of mine, whom I truly love with all my heart, I must ask you a question."

Abdul stopped playing, smiled, and looked up at her. "Yes, my dear?"

"Oh, beloved husband, you have this beautiful instrument that you sit with for hours and hours, playing as your friends do. But my husband, there are many strings on this wonderful instrument and many different places to put your fingers on it—so many different sounds that you could create. Your friends all play such lovely melodies and harmonies on their instruments—a thousand songs come forth from their playing. Why is it that hour after hour, day after day, you keep playing that same string over and over?"

Abdul smiled as he plucked that same string. "My dear wife, that is because all the others are still searching for their own note. I have found mine!"

So go out and find your note.

13

The Application of Different Sounds and Music

In our workshops, many people ask us about different music, particularly music that we use for different situations. We have a fundamental belief that we are all unique vibratory beings. This concept is based on our experiences, research, observations, and intuitive understanding. What works for one person may not work for another. What is perceived as an extraordinary work of art by one critic may be unimpressive to another—in other words, different strokes for different folks. Nevertheless, in this chapter, we present you with basic principles of sound and music to apply in your journey with sound.

In workshops, we ask how many people are allergic to penicillin. Between ten percent and 15 percent of any audience always raise their hands. Sometimes the percentage is even higher. For most of us, if we're very sick with a bacterial infection, penicillin will save our lives. But for a small percentage, it might be detrimental. The same is true with every form of vibration, sound, or music. From our understanding, it is not possible that, given the variety of people and their vibrational rates and eccentricities, any one sound, chemical, food, or substance will have the same effect on everyone.

Sometimes, the percentage of people who have adverse reactions to a particular sound can be very low. For instance, we'll have 99 percent of a population respond favorably to a recording or a sound, but there's always one person who cannot abide the sounds. This may come in the form of a dissatisfied listener or an email from someone asking, "What the heck was that sound I heard? I couldn't stand it."

At our workshops, we give everyone the opportunity of experiencing the Pythagorean tuning forks (discussed in appendix A). This is a positive and enjoyable experience for almost everyone, but occasionally there is a person who has an unpleasant experience. Rather than taking it personally, we acknowledge the uniqueness of every individual and honor that person's experience and move on. The reason for an adverse reaction is always a mystery to us—aside from the fact that each of us is a unique vibratory being.

Once a friend called us after having been sick for a week from receiving a treatment from a sound therapist. Our friend used Jonathan's recording of "Dolphin Dreams" to put himself back into a state of balance. When he reported his experience to the sound therapist who had administered the frequency to him, he was told, "You were so out of balance—that's why you got sick!" Our friend asked our opinion. We said perhaps the frequency he had received was inappropriate and perhaps he should not return to this sonic practitioner. However, he did return, got another dose of the sound, and the same thing happened. He did not return for a third session.

If you react positively to a product—an aroma, color, supplement, sound—it's probably good for you. In particular, if you like a sound and it makes you feel good, continue using it. We recommend that if you begin to have an adverse reaction with a sound, immediately stop using it. While there is the possibility that you are out of balance with that sound, if the adverse reaction continues, there's an equally good chance that the sound is not right for you. Because every person is unique, we like to deal with sounds and music as a subjective, rather than an objective, science.

One could write a book about music that is good for you versus music that is not good for you. Indeed, there are people who have done so. However, this is not our purpose. Nor is it our belief. Given the time, the place, and the need of the individual, we believe that practically any music can potentially have therapeutic effects. On one level, it's all a matter of perspective. When driving late at night, listening to slow, relaxing music that is helpful for inducing sleep may not be good if you want to stay awake. In that situation, stimulating music that acts like sonic caffeine would be more appropriate.

The Psychology of Music

In the 1930s, Carl Seashore developed the psychology of music. Among the areas he explored were people's reactions to different music. He tested many people's responses to music and found that nobody agreed one hundred percent. Probably the highest percentage of similar responses he got to any piece of music was to "Stars and Stripes Forever." Approximately 70 percent of those he tested found this music stimulating. The rest of the audience split their responses between boring and depressing. Seashore was amazed that reactions varied so much.

It seems things have not changed much since then—at least with regard to people and music. So we stress that one person's response to music may be different from another's. That said, we'd like to suggest a few ideas with regard to sound and music.

First, there are some generic psychoacoustic effects that you can usually count on. One of these is that fast music will stimulate your nervous system while slower-paced music will sedate it. If you want to excite someone, use music that is up-tempo, with fast rhythms and a lot of dynamic changes. If you want to use music for relaxation, use slow and gentle music, with a minimum emphasis on rhythm or dynamic changes. For example, music pulsed at around 60 beats per minute will help induce alpha states (8–12 Hz), slowing down heart rate, respiration, and brain waves. Jonathan frequently uses music that is pulsed even slower than that for a number of his meditation and sound healing recordings. Now, if you double those 60 beats to 120 beats, and particularly if you accent the beats, you have good rhythms for movement and dancing.

If your purpose is to relax and slow down, use music that is slow. You don't need to know the beats per minutes to feel the effect of the music. If the music makes you want to boogie, it won't be useful in creating a sedative effect. If you want music for aerobics, use fast music. If you are looking for exercise music, slow music will not assist you since your nervous system (as well as your muscular system) will want to entrain with the slow music. This is not good if you're trying to burn calories or tone tissue.

Choosing Music

Choose music that is congruent with your activity. If you're trying to relax before bed, slow music will usually work best. Do you want a gentle, quiet meal? Listen to music that's not too fast, too distracting, or too rhythmic. Don't play upbeat music! And don't raise the volume too loud because loud music (and loud sounds in general) causes the fight-or-flight response, raising your heartbeat, respiration, and brain waves, and can induce stress, particularly when listened to for long periods of time.

Loud sounds can be addictive because they stimulate the nervous system and release adrenaline. Many times the rush one experiences from music may be due to its volume rather than one's emotional response to it. This can be the case with any type of music, including classical. Of course, loud, fast music is the most effective at stimulating your nervous system because you get a double dose of psychoacoustic effects from rhythms and volume. This is great for staying alert at night while you're driving, but such sounds are not as beneficial while you're having a relaxing meal.

The next time you're in a fast-food restaurant listen to the music. Odds are it will be up-tempo, probably pop music. This is most often not accidental since the people who own these restaurants have some knowledge of which type of music makes people get in and get out the quickest.

Very few people are aware of the power of music, and even fewer people are aware of the relationship between the music they are listening to and the activities they are engaged in. We have at times suggested that people create their own "Sonic Prescriptions," writing down specific activities they frequently engage in and then contemplating what type of music they should listen to that best relates to this activity.

Compromise is an important part of using sound for tantra in relationship. It's wonderful if you have the same tastes, but this is rare. Most probably if your musical tastes are the same as your partner's, other of your tastes will differ. This may be a gift, for most of us would grow bored if our partners shared our exact tastes. We would also not have the opportunity for growth, which occurs when we need to experience things that we normally wouldn't encounter. Even if you don't like your partner's choice of music, by practicing the fluidity we've suggested, perhaps you'll be able to compromise and find music you can both listen to together. It may not be your favorite music, but at least it may be something to which you can both resonate.

Note that while we are indeed unique vibratory beings, there seems to be something about musical tastes and age, although we can't say for sure what it is, except perhaps that as we grow older our nervous systems and metabolism change. Once we could do homework with the radio blaring Top 40 hits, now we need either silence or ambient music to concentrate.

This does not mean, however, that we recommend that young people listen to pop music while studying. Research indicates that music that is not distracting (usually instrumental, without vocal lyrics or a strong melodic recognition factor) may be the best to assist in the learning process. Some have suggested that Mozart is the best for studying, some recommend Bach; classical to light jazz, ambient music such as New Age, or even environmental sounds are effective in enhancing learning. These types of music are not particularly distracting; they can play in the background, minimally stimulating our ears and nervous systems without pulling much attention away from what we are studying.

Our purpose is simply to point out differences that manifest musically between different age groups. It reminds us of when our parents first heard rock and roll; if you were a teenager at the time of Elvis or the Beatles your reaction was probably very different from that of your parents or grandparents. Certainly, some of these differences were cultural and sociological, while others were neurological, hormonal, or metabolic. No doubt, there are also emotional, mental, and spiritual reasons why we respond differently to music.

The Iso Principle

The word "iso" means equal. This term indicates a technique used by therapists to match different behaviors and induce different moods in their clients. A therapist who works with music will first find the appropriate music that mirrors the mood of the client, and then will gradually change the music to better assist the client in the healing process. For example, if a client were sad and depressed, a therapist might first start with slow, downbeat music in order to help him express his emotions, then gradually raise the tempo of the music until it helped induce a more contented state in the client.

The iso principle may help explain why one person might not

react to music the same way as another—even if the music is encoded with various sonic entrainment frequencies. As we have discussed, sound affects our brain and nervous system. We have noted many of the remarkable discoveries in this field, yet despite knowledge of psychoacoustics, it is not possible to determine exactly how music will affect any one person. If someone is nervous and stressed-out, gentle, relaxing music encoded with entrainment frequencies may not work for them. They may simply be too tense to be affected. It may be necessary to first use music that reflects their nervous state—fast, frenetic music—and then begin to bring in slower music to change the nervous system of the individual, ultimately calming and relaxing them.

Sound is an extraordinary, powerful tool, but it is not magic. In 1989, Jonathan presented his research paper on "Sonic Entrainment" at the International Society for Music Medicine's meeting at the Eisenhower Center in Rancho Mirage, California. The paper was on how scientific knowledge of certain closely related frequencies could cause the predominant lobes of the brain to entrain with the sounds.

The first question came from a doctor: "How can you differentiate between what you have just described—this sonic entrainment—and brainwashing?"

Jonathan replied that sonic entrainment is neither immutable nor unstoppable. Someone who wishes to experience shifts in their brain waves can do so through the process described. However, if someone is fearful or unwilling or that person's nervous system is resonating at too great a difference in frequency, then sonic entrainment will have little or no effect.

We are being entrained all the time by different frequencies—often by many everyday objects generating sounds or electrical waves, including the television. Just because our brain waves may be resonating to a particular frequency does not mean we've had a change of consciousness. The act of watching television frequently puts people into an alpha state (which is no doubt why people often find themselves very relaxed). However, being a couch potato whose brain is operating at 8 Hz (or whatever level) is very different from being a Zen monk whose brain is operating at the same frequency.

In other words, the difference between entrainment and brainwashing is that brainwashing attempts to instill specific content that will have a permanent effect. This is important to understand. While there is a relationship between states of consciousness and brain wave activity, it is not a one-to-one correlation. What you are doing with your consciousness during this time—where your mind, your visualizations, your thought processes go during this time—is of utmost importance. Again, here we have "Frequency + Intent."

More on "Frequency + Intent"

We believe nothing in this book will be one hundred percent effective for everyone. There are always exceptions. Here is an example: If you were trapped in a room for hours with specific frequencies boomed at you by loudspeakers, you probably would experience massive, perhaps even detrimental, changes in your neurological system. However, this type of neurological effect cannot result from using the self-created vocal techniques we described in this book. With regard to recorded music, despite advances in sound technology and psychoacoustics, it is not possible for normal playback systems (including headphones) to have such power that an individual would be sonically "swept away" if that were not her desire.

When Jonathan was researching *Healing Sounds,* he sent a questionnaire to dozens of well-known people in the field of sound and music for healing—musicians, doctors, healers, and scientists located in various countries.

The questionnaire asked what types of music these people used for different activities, such as getting up in the morning, exercising, eating, etc. Despite his awareness of the uniqueness of everyone, particularly in how we respond to musical choices, Jonathan was surprised to find nearly every answer was different. It convinced him even more of our individuality. There was no consensus about music for any activity. When asked what sort of music was used to wake up in the morning, some people listened to gentle nature sounds such as the sounds of birds singing; others listened to flutes or light classical music or rock music. Two doctors from Germany who lived in different parts of the country and did not know each other both listened to German marching bands to wake up.

Creating a "Sonic Prescription" for yourself can be useful for realizing what types of music you like for different activities. Here are some categories to consider.

What music do you listen to when you:

- wake up?
- exercise or engage in physical activity?
- study or do mental activity?
- cook or clean?
- relax or prepare for sleep?
- drive in your car?
- engage in lovemaking?

- use the computer?
- want to be happy?
- feel sad?
- feel scared?
- want to chase the blues away?
- dance?
- meditate?
- eat a meal?

Most of these categories can be broken up into two groups: music that stimulates, such as fast tempo music that you might dance to; and music that sedates, such as gentle environmental sounds that you might use to help you sleep.

Assessing the different types of music you use for different activities can be effective for helping you understand your own specific responses to music. Start observing yourself, your musical likes and dislikes, and see what sort of music resonates with you. If you have a partner, have them start observing and noting this information. That way when you're together, you can compare notes. See if you agree or disagree on a piece of music for a particular circumstance; then at least you can compromise and find something that works for both of you.

We have encountered individuals who were adamant (and rigid) about their likes and dislikes in music. Some were unwilling to take a step away from what they consider to be "good" music and sometimes got distressed, even angry, at the idea of being exposed to other music. "Give me Beethoven or give me death!" Part of being fluid in relationship is compromise. It is our hope that through the exercises and information in this book you will acquire tools and skills to help you grow through these issues.

After you have made your selections, contemplate why the music works for you. Do the rhythm and pulsations being generated stimulate or sedate your nervous system? Or is it because you heard a piece of music at some time in your life and whenever you hear this music, it brings back that memory? Emotional entrainment with music is common, and it is important in understanding the use of music to influence your physical activities and consciousness. As you observe how and why different music affects you, you might have some interesting insights about yourself and your life.

Andi is a great advocate of writing down thoughts, ideas, feelings, emotions—anything and everything relevant to her. We suggest beginning a journal in which you record different songs and their effects on you. You might also want to journal your thoughts and feelings with any of the exercises and experiences in this book.

Become a sonic explorer and chart new territories of music by yourself or with a partner. There are hundreds of thousands of songs and many genres of music. Create your Sonic Prescription and discover music to enhance whatever activity you or your partner are engaged in. Just as the Buddha discovered the Middle Way, so can you and your partner, even if you are musically miles apart in taste. You can discover a musical middle way that will allow you to be in harmony and peace together.

And in the End

Musicians, philosophers, and spiritual teachers from all different paths, from the Beatles to Tibetan Buddhists, have told us that more than money, fame, or deeds, the most important aspect of life—that which matters most at the end of life—is the love that we have created and the love we have received. When most people are lying on their deathbed awaiting passage to the Other Side, they're not concerned with the number of hours they have logged onto the Internet or spent in the office, but with how much love has been given and how much love has been received. Love is, apparently, all you need!

By love, we mean the heartfelt tenderness of unconditional love, loving-kindness and nonjudgment of others. There are many different forms of love—perhaps the greatest that we know involves unconditional love, what many call compassion. We highly recommend

Unconditional Love by Ed and Deb Shapiro (Time Warner, 2003) to delve into this important subject.

In workshops, we frequently use different mantras to manifest loving-kindness and compassion. In particular, we often teach the Tibetan Buddhist chant "Om Mani Padme Hum." This is a chant to invoke the bodhisattva of compassion, Avalokitesvara. We also facilitate "Tara Trance Dances" in which participants, while drumming and dancing, chant the mantra "Om Tara Tu Tare Ture Svaha" to Tara, the Tibetan goddess of compassion. We have found that when experiencing sound for extended periods of time (as you, no doubt, already have through the exercises in this book), not only do our heart rate, respiration, and brain waves change, but our consciousness changes as well.

Since everything in the universe is in a state of vibration and everything is a waveform, compassion is a waveform. So are the different deities and beings who represent compassion. During workshops we often pass around a picture of Avalokitesvara while describing the different attributes of this deity and the "Om Mani Padme Hum" chant; or we distribute a picture of Tara, talking of her attributes and chant. We tell participants that while both pictures are depictions of the bodhisattva of compassion, this by no means limits us to what we can visualize or, in fact, what may manifest for us during the exercise.

In China, the masculine Avalokitesvara has been transformed into the female entity Quan Yin. Recently, we saw an old Japanese painting of Quan Yin, and she had a moustache, so perhaps this being's gender is still in question. In Tibetan Buddhism, the female aspect of Avalokitesvara is Tara. She is his consort, said to have been born out of a tear of compassion shed by him. From our perspective, however, Tara is simply an embodiment of a hundred different forms of the divine goddess of compassion known in a hundred different traditions by a hundred different names. In Native traditions, she is the Earth Goddess. In Western traditions, she is perceived as Great Mother or the Blessed Virgin Mary. Here in the West, her masculine counterpart may be understood as that most compassionate of beings we call Jesus. And for many, Mary Magdalene is considered the wife/mate of Jesus, as well as his main apostle.

The energy of compassion as a waveform is frequently anthropomorphized by many different cultures and spiritual traditions of this planet into many different names of many different beings, but essentially the energy is the same. Its energy, whether attributed to Jesus or Tara or Mary or whomever, is transformative.

From our Western perspective, we understand compassion as meaning unconditional love. Yet, for many, this concept is foreign, so we suggest loving-kindness, tenderness, or appreciation instead. Why is unconditional love so difficult to understand? Perhaps because our experiences of love have been so conditional: I'll love you if you . . . do your homework, get on the football team, make lots of money, become a doctor, call me on Sundays, cook good food for me, give me great sex, do my laundry.

We could go on about the "ifs" that exist with conditional love. The love that is selfless—unconditional love—is alien to most of us. Thus at the end of our chant of "Om Mani Padme Hum" (the "Mani"), as we sit in silence and meditation, it is not unusual for many to experience forgiveness. This seems an essential step in manifesting compassion and unconditional love. Usually, this forgiveness is first generated toward oneself, then toward others.

Previously, we discussed how many of us carry emotional wounding from our childhoods, associated with feeling we are bad, unworthy, guilty, undeserving, or unlovable. As a result, we may have low self-esteem or a poor self-image.

What is important is that being able to generate forgiveness to oneself is a crucial first step in healing these wounds. Using these sound techniques with the intention of forgiveness to manifest compassion toward ourselves and others is a helpful tool to initiate this.

The lack of self-love that many of us have seems to be connected to our feelings of separation from the Divine (God/Goddess/whatever you want to call this energy). One of the benefits of working with tantra of sound is that it can undo the barriers between our self and the sacred. It gives us a hotline to the Divine for instant access to the web of life. As we become more aware of the love that unites us, we become conscious of the sameness of us and all that is. While we are all unique, we are also aspects of the Divine.

Thus utilizing sound to manifest loving-kindness has great healing ability for ourselves and others as it creates unity. After chanting the "Mani," we lead people in a brief meditation. In it, they imagine themselves as divine beings who have the ability to generate compassion and loving-kindness toward others. We first generate this healing energy for someone we love, then for someone we don't know, then for someone with whom we have difficulty.

This last projection is the most difficult and yet the most important. It is easy to generate kindness to someone we know, and not too difficult to someone we don't know. But to generate loving-kindness and healing to someone with whom we've had bad encounters is an accomplishment.

His Holiness, the 14th Dalai Lama, once stated that the Chinese have been his greatest teachers. Said to be the incarnation of Avalokitesvara, the Dalai Lama's purpose is to generate compassion. If you examine the lives of various spiritual teachers, you will find that they all taught the power of love and compassion.

Vowels as Mantras Sound Bites

As we bring the material in this book to a close, we would be remiss if we did not include one last exercise that may be the most relevant of any we have presented. What we call a "sound bite" is a version of a previous, much longer exercise. We have found that due to time constraints and making excuses, many will experiment with the exercises in this book, but just once and that's all. Because sound is such a powerful tool and we believe it is important for all of us to resonate with sound on a daily basis, we have created this very brief sound exercise that is easy to practice every day. The two of us frequently use the "there's no time" excuse, so we created this exercise as much for ourselves as for others. Here is a shortened version of the Vowels as Mantras exercise. It is effective and easily done, particularly when you add to this exercise the intention to balance and align your chakras.

As always, find a note that is comfortable for you. To begin, focus your attention on your root chakra and sound the *UH* while feeling this chakra being balanced and aligned. Now, on your next breath, focus your attention on your sacral chakra and sound the *OOO* on this same note while feeling this chakra being balanced and aligned. On your next breath, focus on the navel chakra, and on the same note, sound the *OH*. Next, focus on the heart with an *AH*— same note. Next, focus on your throat center with an *EYE*. Next breath, focus on your third eye with an *AYE*. Finally, focus on your crown and sound forth with an *EEE* to balance and align this chakra with all the others.

Allocate one breath per vowel sound. To complete one round of this exercise might take a minute, yet it can make all the difference in the world. It will not give you the experience that the 20-minute version does—we doubt you will be thrown into another dimension for meetings with remarkable beings—but this exercise will do several things. It will (1) remind you that you have chakras, (2) remind you of the power of sound, (3) remind you of your ability to shift and move energy using your voice, and (4) assist you in setting an intention for the day or a segment of time.

One of the wonderful things about this exercise is that it can be done anywhere, anytime. We do this exercise at least once a day, in the morning, but we often do it more. For those who find it difficult to create the space of even a half-hour to make sounds, we offer you this "sound bite" exercise as an alternative to making no sounds at all.

Incidentally, you can do this exercise several times, bringing the energy up your chakras, focusing on each chakra with one breath/vowel sound. Try sounding all the vowels for the entire sequence with just one or two breaths. The more you practice this, the more you will be amazed at the power of your projected sound to resonate your chakras, regardless of the time you're spending on making the sound.

There are variations on the Vowels as Mantras sound bite, which include sounding each vowel sound on a different note (a major scale, for example, as we suggested in previous chapters). Another alternative is to reverse the order, starting with the *EEE* sound at the crown center and working your way down, ending up at the root chakra with the *UH*. This is highly recommended.

Regardless of the variation, we suggest you do this practical exercise every day. It will take only a minute. You can be brushing your hair and do this without missing a brush stroke, or you can be putting on your shoes and remember this exercise and sound forth. Ideally, we prefer that you take a moment, enter sacred space, and do this exercise. There have been times when we're about to walk out the door and suddenly stop, take a deep breath, and sound our chakras. It can make all the difference in the world.

Closing Thoughts

In order to enhance your relationships or to bring wanted changes into your life, begin with yourself. Be kind to yourself. Accept and love yourself just as you are at this very moment. Know that if you could have done things differently in the past, you would have. When you work with self-created sacred sounds every day with the intention of love and inner peace, you will begin to feel changes. From our perspective, it is impossible to work consciously with sound without a change in consciousness occurring. Thus we encourage you to explore the world of sound and incorporate it into your daily life. It will only make things better, evoking harmony and balance in you.

In conclusion, we would like to thank you for joining us on this journey through the tantra of sound. It has been our desire to create an educational and entertaining book, one that is readable, user-friendly, and easy to understand. We trust we have succeeded. For those of you who want to explore this field in depth, there are many books and articles on the subjects of sound and tantra available from many sources, including the Internet. We have included some of these sources in appendix B.

However, further resources are not necessary to begin your personal exploration of sound. You have everything you need right here. Practice your sonic exercises with intention and mindfulness—that's all it takes. How you use the material in this book is as dependent on your intention as the sounds you make. We ask that you come from your heart as well as from your head. Between the two, wisdom and compassion will meet through the sounds you create. May joyous sounds resonate with you always!

Appendices

Appendix A

Tools of the Trade

This book has focused mainly on the use of the voice as an instrument of self-transformation and healing. The voice is the most powerful vehicle for projecting the energies of compassion and love. Yet there are some simple instruments—tools of the trade—that can provide a sonic "jump start" for sound explorers, healers, and practitioners. These include tuning forks, quartz crystal bowls, Tibetan bowls, and *ting-shas* (Tibetan bells). There are many other instruments also available. We have focused on these four because of their popularity, power, and affordability.

Tuning Forks

Of all the tools currently available, probably the most popular are tuning forks. There are many websites devoted to the different types

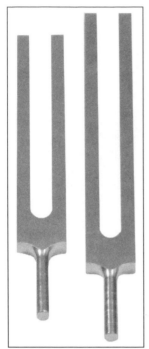

Figure 16 A set of tuning forks.

of tuning forks and the many ways of using them. There are tuning forks specifically created for work on the body. There are also tuning forks that feature different frequencies, modes, and scales. We concentrate on two: (1) the Pythagorean tuning forks, cut to the ratio of 2:3 (the relationship between the two frequencies of the tuning forks), developed by John Beaulieu, and (2) the DnA# tuning forks, cut to the ratio of 8:13, developed by Jonathan Goldman.

Pythagorean Tuning Forks

Pythagorean tuning forks are a new way of using sound to resonate the body, brain, and etheric fields. They were developed by John Beaulieu, N.D., Ph.D., author of *Music and Sound in the Healing Arts.*

These tuning forks are used in pairs because it is possible to create an exact interval and ratio between the two that have specific effects on the body and, in particular, the nervous system. Single tuning forks will create only one note. Used together, a pair of tuning forks cut to different frequencies can create many different ratios. Each of these ratios may have very specific effects on us.

Pythagorean tuning forks have the frequencies of 256 Hz (cycles per second, which is the note C) and 384 Hz (the note G). The ratio that these two harmonically related frequencies of 256 Hz and 384 Hz create is 2:3. The musical interval whose ratio is 2:3 is called the perfect fifth. (An interval is the distance between two frequencies.) Listening to this interval is relaxing and balancing and is considered the most harmonious musical relationship that exists. This ratio of 2:3 is sacred in many traditions, based on an understanding of the relationship between mathematics, music, and the cosmos. Legend tells us that Pythagoras believed the ratio of 2:3 to be therapeutic and transformative.

These forks create a calmness and tranquility, and balance the hemispheres of the brain, reducing brain wave activity and inducing relaxation. Many users feel they balance the aura and release blocked energy. Frequently, people experience many other positive experiences from using the forks.

According to Dr. Beaulieu, one of the great pioneers in this field, who writes in *Music and Sound* (Station Hill, 1987): "When we listen to the tuning forks, our vestibular system via the semicircular canals [in the ears] reproportions our body based on the natural ratios of the tuning forks. During the listening process, our physical body repostures itself in alignment with the interval created by the tuning forks. During the process, our nervous system via the right and left hemispheres of the brain comes into balance."

Dr. Beaulieu adds: "This special interval is known in music as a perfect fifth. Lao Tzu referred to this interval as the sound of universal harmony between the forces of Yin and Yang. In India, the fifth is believed to create a sound through which Shiva calls Shakti to the dance of life. Apollo, the Greek Sun God of Music and Healing, plucked the fifth on his sacred lyre to call dolphin messengers to Delphi."

To use the tuning forks, hold them by their stems and tap them gently, then bring one to each ear, keeping them several inches away from the ears. The tuning forks may be tapped on the kneecaps or tapped together (at least a foot away from the ear). Each method produces a slightly different sound, though the inherent 2:3 ratio remains. The tones of tuning forks vary, but last for approximately half a minute.

Experiment. Use the tuning forks on yourself, friends, clients. They can produce remarkable experiences. Therapists frequently use them to calm and balance clients before or after sessions. When the nervous system comes into alignment, the body and energy fields frequently follow, repatterning with the sacred ratio of the tuning forks.

You can use these tuning forks on yourself, by yourself. It is wonderful to have someone use them on you and allow yourself the luxury of being tuned. You can exchange tunings with each other; both of you will benefit from this pleasurable and healing experience. Try humming or sounding with the tuning forks. Have fun using them and remember that they are tools for self-healing and transformation.

These tuning forks are wonderful accompaniments for

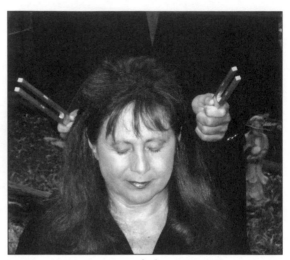

Figure 17 Using tuning forks on a partner.

you to use before, during, or after toning with your voice to balance your chakras. They are also wonderful vehicles if you feel out of harmony. You'll be surprised how quickly disharmonious energies can be dissipated by the use of tuning forks.

We particularly like the aluminum tuning forks, not only because they are powerful, effective sonic tools, but because they are lightweight and easy to carry.

DnA# Tuning Forks

The DnA# tuning forks present a new musical ratio developed by Jonathan Goldman. They are named in such a manner because this particular set of tuning forks uses frequencies found within the notes of D and A#. This specific ratio has been described as harmonizing our DNA, so we have fondly named this set the "DnA#" tuning forks. These two forks manifest the ratio of 8:13 (the relationship between the two frequencies of the tuning forks). The interval of this ratio is generically called the minor sixth, but is not found in contemporary music.

The DnA# tuning forks can be used in the same way as the 2:3 tuning forks. They are balancing and relaxing and they seem to enhance spiritual initiation and activation. When tapped together, they produce a sound that many have called "angelic."

Some people, when they hear this ratio, report to us that it feels as if they are "home." Others have found that the sounds of these forks create an energetic spiraling effect. This is not surprising because the 8:13 ratio of these tuning forks represents an outer spiral of the Fibonacci series, an important mathematical sequence discovered in the thirteenth century by an Italian mathematician. This mathematical sequence is one in which the addition of the two previous numbers creates the next number. It goes: 1, 1, 2, 3, 5, **8, 13,** 21, 34, 55, 89, 144, 233, 377, 610, 987 and continues into infinity. Called the "Divine Ratio," the proportions created by the numbers are found throughout nature in the growth patterns of plants, animals, and even humans. Almost any spiral found in nature, such as the shape of a nautilus shell or the cochlea of the ear, is an example of this proportion. Thus the spiraling effects reported to us made sense because people may have been hearing the Divine Ratio manifested as sound. Many find the 8:13 tuning forks activate new levels of consciousness, and are particularly useful for the tantra of sound. For those wishing further information about the Fibonacci series, we recommend *The Golden Ratio: The Story of Phi* by Mario Livio (Broadway Books, 2003).

Quartz Crystal Bowls

Among the most popular sonic tools are quartz crystal bowls made from 99.992 percent pure crushed quartz. The bowls are either clear or frosted and come in sizes ranging from six to 24 inches in diameter. The bowls emit a pure tone when activated with a mallet or wand. The larger bowls are more reverberant, the tone lingering longer because of the size and amount of crystal. The clear bowls, somewhat more expensive, are more readily available in smaller sizes. In recent years, many new varieties, shapes, and styles of crystal bowls have become available.

When these bowls first appeared in the sound healing field, few knew that they were the remnants of scientific laboratories—discarded containers that were used to grow quartz crystals for computers. Someone discovered that these bowls produced a powerful tone when struck or rubbed around the rim with a rubber mallet, and began making them available to the public in the 1980s.

The sounds are remarkable. Whether they came about as an inadvertent offspring of crystal growth in scientific laboratories, or if they really are the rediscovery of an ancient Atlantean artifact, probably does not matter. They're wonderful sonic healing tools.

More and more practitioners of crystal bowls have appeared. There are even medical doctors who have acknowledged their therapeutic value. The bowls come in a variety of sizes, shapes, and colors, in the notes C, D, E, F, G, A, B, which many believe correspond with the frequencies of the chakras.

Quartz crystals seem to work as amplifiers of intent, and thus these quartz crystal bowls can amplify intent through sound. They are wonderful healing implements to use in ceremony to set an intention. We often use our crystal bowls when toning together in meditation and/or for a specific intention. They can also clear an area of negative energy.

Rubber ball mallets or suede-covered wands are rubbed around the rims of the bowls to create the sound. The sound of each bowl is different, and your preference will determine your choice. When struck by a rubber ball mallet, the tone of a crystal bowl can last for a minute or two. When played using the rubber ball mallet around the edge of the bowl, the tone can last indefinitely. The sound is similar to the glass harmonic, or to the sound that occurs when you run your fingers around a fine glass goblet and hear it resonate with a pure, crystalline tone. Each practitioner has a unique style of sounding the bowls; some will move the wand or mallet clockwise for specific intentions, while others prefer a counterclockwise motion, or a combination.

From our experience, the purity and power of crystal bowls are impressive. They generate excellent sound and are marvelous at amplifying our intent on the sound. The tone of just one bowl can balance and align any or all of the chakras; this is particularly true for those who sound with clear intention.

Figure 18 Quartz crystal bowl.

Many crystal bowl practitioners have a variety of different bowls that they use specifically for particular chakras and purposes. We are currently experimenting with using two crystal bowls cut to very exact musical ratios, such as 2:3 or 8:13. We have found that while having several bowls for specific purposes is wonderful, having just one bowl by itself can be sufficient for almost any type of vibrational work. However, once you have established your resonance with a crystal bowl, get as many crystal bowls as you like.

The cost of crystal bowls varies depending on size and substance. Some of the latest developments in crystal bowl technology have produced bowls made out of rose quartz or moldavite; some have stems you can hold, which makes them easier to handle.

We love crystal bowls; they are one of the most powerful sonic tools on the planet. We caution, however, that a crystal bowl is as fragile as a glass goblet and is difficult to transport unless you have a special case for it.

Tibetan Bowls

From Tibet, Nepal, and Bhutan come these exquisite bowls. The older bowls are made of seven metals—gold, silver, mercury, copper, iron, tin, and lead—which are melted together, poured and cooled as plates, and then formed into bowls by hundreds of hammer blows. The origin of the bowls is shrouded in mystery, but they seem to

Figure 19 Tibetan bowl.

come from the Tibetan Buddhist traditions, handmade by monks chanting mantras into the metals they molded. These Tibetan bowls produce beautiful tones excellent for clearing energy and creating sacred space. The bowls have healing application as the tones produced by them help remove disharmony from our subtle bodies, chakras, and physical body.

Most Tibetan bowls are approximately four to six inches in diameter and are sounded by striking them or rubbing a wooden stick along the rim to make them "sing," producing a beautiful tone. There are, of course, larger Tibetan bowls—some with a diameter of over one foot. Most of these larger bowls are old, heavy, and expensive. When struck by a wooden stick, a Tibetan bowl produces a tone that lasts for a minute (although we have heard recordings of larger ancient bowls whose tones last for several minutes from just one strike).

When played with the wooden stick along the rim, the tones, of course, last for as long as they are played. The bowls produce several tones at the same time, and when multiple bowls are played together, the tones interface and synergize with each other.

Jonathan once worked with a chiropractor using kinesiology to test Tibetan bowls as well as tuning forks for their beneficial effects. They found that, with individual tuning forks, the specific frequencies seemed to vary from person to person in terms of what worked best. However, every Tibetan bowl tested was beneficial for every person tested.

Similar to crystal bowls, Tibetan bowls may be struck and sounded and brought near the person who needs healing; or put the bowl directly on the area of the body of the person and then strike it. In this way, the vibrations of the Tibetan bowl will go directly into the person's body. (This is a method that usually does not work well with crystal bowls, especially the large ones, which are too heavy to place on a person's body.)

People use many different Tibetan bowls in a healing session, assigning a particular bowl to a particular chakra. We would like to suggest that one Tibetan bowl in the hands of a conscious sounder can be enough. Using a Tibetan bowl to create sacred space before, during, or after a session of toning your chakras is highly recommended.

We like to travel with at least one Tibetan bowl. If packed in between some clothes in a suitcase, Tibetan bowls transport well.

Ting-Shas

Though Tibetan bells, or *ting-shas*, have been used in Buddhist meditation practice for centuries, they are probably the least well-known of the tools. These instruments are struck together to create sounds that calm the mind and induce relaxation. The two disc-shaped bells, rung together, are slightly out of tune with each other. The different tones between the two bells produce a very slow frequency that can entrain the brain to an alpha or theta waveform. For example, if one bell were creating a frequency of 300 Hz (or cycles per second) and the other bell were creating a frequency of 305 Hz, it would create a third frequency of 5 Hz—the difference between the two frequencies. This 5 Hz frequency falls within the bandwidth of theta brain wave activity. The science of psychoacoustics has shown that the low sonic frequencies such as in this example can cause our brain waves to synchronize with those frequencies. We have found that most *ting-shas* create a difference in tone of between 4 and 8 Hz. This falls exactly within the range of the brain wave activity created during meditation. It is little wonder that Tibetan bells are experiencing an increase in popularity as tools for greater relaxation and reduction of stress.

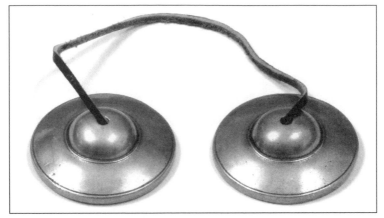

Figure 20 A set of *ting-shas* or Tibetan bells.

In Tibetan Buddhism, *ting-shas* are used in rituals. We have found that simply tapping them together induces relaxation. This may be due to the deep alpha and theta waves they produce as well as the clarity and beauty of their sounds. Ringing them together seems to help announce to our psyche that we are about to enter a sacred time and space.

The tone of *ting-shas* is at first powerful, almost piercing; then it lessens and fades, though the overall sound may last for a minute. Due to the purity of their sound, *ting-shas* can be used for clearing imbalanced energies in the auric field, or even the physical body. In addition, they are excellent as vehicles to summon people or get an audience's attention at a meeting. They are lightweight and easy to carry.

Appendix B

Recommendations

There are many books and recordings that are relevant to the field of sound and tantra. Here are a few of our favorites.

Books

Category: Sound and Music

Cymatics: A Study of Wave Phenomena and Vibration (combined vols. I and II), by Dr. Hans Jenny (MACROMEDIA, 2001). An extraordinary book of breathtaking photographs by Swiss medical doctor Hans Jenny demonstrating the ability of sound to create form. This is proof of the power of sound to affect physical matter.

The Healing Forces of Music, by Randall McClellan, Ph.D. (iUniverse, August 1, 2000). Published some years ago, the information in this book is still valid and relevant today. Randall's book contains much valuable and important material on the history, theory, and practice of different systems that utilize sound and music for healing and transformation.

Healing Sounds, by Jonathan Goldman (Inner Traditions, 2002). Considered a cutting-edge classic in the field of sound healing, this book contains much information on the spiritual and scientific aspects of sound healing. In particular, it focuses on the use of voice as a healing instrument. Also recommended: the same author's *Shifting Frequencies.*

Music and Sound in the Healing Arts, by John Beaulieu (Station Hill Press, 1987). This important book contains much valuable information on the therapeutic and transformational uses of sound and music. It includes mantras, tuning forks, voice energetics, and much more. John is a great teacher and pioneer in the field of sound healing. We highly recommend this book.

Music: Physician for Times to Come, edited by Don Campbell (Quest Books, 2000). This is an important anthology by many diverse musicians, scientists, and spiritual teachers focusing on the healing use of sound and music. Varied approaches on the subject make for fascinating reading.

The Power of Sound, by Joshua Leeds (Inner Traditions, 2001). Joshua's book focuses more on the importance of healthy auditory functions, the process of hearing, and how sounds can assist in learning, communication, and social interactions. In particular, the subject of psychoacoustics (how sound affects our nervous system) is explored in depth.

Toning: The Creative Power of the Voice, by Laurel Elizabeth Keyes (DeVorss & Co., 1973). This is the original work that, for many, initiated the extraordinary path of using self-created sound for healing and transformation. A user-friendly book, it is considered a classic in the field of sound healing.

Category: Body Energetics, Spiritual Mysteries, Tantra

The Book of Secrets, by Deepak Chopra (Harmony 2004). An extraordinary book in which the 15 spiritual secrets for enlightenment are revealed. Dr. Chopra brings to light the existence of a universal intelligence that operates beneath the visible surface of life. You'll discover insights and exercises that can transform consciousness, leading to the ecstasy of enlightenment.

Hands of Light, by Barbara Ann Brennan (Bantam, 1988). A look at the field of bioenergetic healing, with specific techniques for expanding tools of healing, seeing auras, understanding psychodynamics and the human energy field, and spiritual healing. This is a detailed study of chakras and the subtle body and how they are connected to a person's health and well-being.

The Isaiah Effect, by Gregg Braden (Three Rivers Press, 2001). Gregg is a wonderful writer, researcher, and purveyor of ancient wisdom. In this book, he decodes the lost science of prayer and prophecy, exploring the technology of a lost mode of prayer and presenting a dazzling new interpretation of the key prophecy from the Dead Sea Scrolls.

Kundalini: Yoga for the West, by Swami Sivananda Radha (Shambhala, 1978). This book focuses on the chakras from the classic Hindu tradition. For those wishing to gain an immense knowledge of these energy centers, the *bija* mantras, and how they can be utilized to assist as forces of evolution, this book is highly recommended.

Tantra in Tibet, by His Holiness the Dalai Lama, Tsong-ka-pa, and Jeffrey Hopkins (Snow Lion, 1987). Some important writings on the Tibetan perspective of tantra. This book contains in-depth source material from important writers on the subject of tantra.

Vibrational Medicine, by Richard Gerber, M.D. (Bear & Co., 2001). Dr. Gerber explores the benefits of many different therapies that utilize different vibratory medicines including homeopathy, acupuncture, color and light healing, and magnetic healing, among other therapies. One of the original sourcebooks with regard to this, it has been recently updated to include material on sound.

Category: Relationships

Conscious Loving, by Gay and Kathlyn Hendricks (Bantam, 1992). From a husband and wife team of psychologists who live what they teach, here you'll find powerful techniques for transforming relationships. They have developed strategies to help create a vital partnership and enhance the energy, creativity, and happiness of each individual. Also recommended: the same authors' *Conscious Breathing.*

The Dance of Intimacy, by Harriet Lerner (Perennial, 1990). This sensible self-help book draws on family-systems therapy in recommending thoughtful "self-focus" for people stuck in difficult relationships with either mates or families. Lerner emphasizes that "a truly intimate relationship is one in which we can be who we are, which means being open about ourselves."

Getting the Love You Want, by Harville Hendrix (Owl Books, 2001). An innovator and leader in the field of couples counseling, Hendrix developed Imago Relationship Therapy. This combines many different disciplines including the behavioral sciences, depth psychology, cognitive therapy, and Gestalt therapy. The information and exercises combine to give the reader valuable tools in healing relationships.

Healing the Child Within, by Charles Whitfield (HCI, 1987). This thoughtful and informative book brings cutting-edge information on the concept of the wounded "inner child." The "child within" refers to that part of each of us that is ultimately alive, energetic, creative, and fulfilled; it is our real self, who we truly are. It's easy to understand and digest this exceptional book.

Homecoming: Reclaiming and Championing Your Inner Child, by John Bradshaw (Bantam, 1992). In this guide to understanding and mourning the damage done to the inner child, John Bradshaw shares important information that will inspire you and provide insights that can lead you down a path of self-acceptance and self-love through healing the childhood hurts of wounded adults.

Unconditional Love, by Ed and Deb Shapiro (Time Warner, 2003). The Shapiros are clear teachers who walk their talk with regard to relationships, spirituality, and life. This book is a practical and inspiring blend of the traditions of the compassionate wisdom of the East, using the paths of Buddhism and Yoga as accessible forms for meditation. Wonderful for developing an open heart!

Music by Jonathan Goldman

Celestial Reiki, by Jonathan and Laraaji. With his celestial zither, Laraaji is one of the pioneers of ambient music. He and Jonathan create hypnotic trance music, with zither, synthesizer, guitar, and bells, that enhances all forms of tantric activity. For creating deep relaxation and stress reduction.

Celestial Yoga. More than an hour of transcendent music with three instrumental pieces created to assist in a yogic practice, to enhance any form of bodywork or healing, such as reiki, or to serve as background music to relieve stress. Great for those tantric times when you want to experience unity. With synthesizers, guitars, choral voices, bells, and zither.

Chakra Chants. This combines the sacred vowels with *bija* mantras, Pythagorean tuning forks, elemental and Shabd yoga sounds, male and female choral voices, and much more. An hour-long sacred sound experience that has been an award-winning bestseller for many years. Designed for meditation and deep sound healing, it initiates a new level of therapeutic sound. This recording is the 1999 Visionary Award winner for both Best Healing and Meditation Album as well as Album of the Year. It continues to be in the top ten healing albums.

ChakraDance. Combines Jonathan Goldman's world-renowned chakra tones and chants with electronic and techno dance rhythms. This fusion of ancient sacred sounds, including mantras and chants with psychoacoustics and modern beats, will get your feet stomping and your chakras resonating. Many tell us that this recording is perfect for tantric ritual! Created for the young in body, mind, or spirit.

The Divine Name. Working with spiritual scientist Gregg Braden, Jonathan has created an extraordinary, groundbreaking sonic work using the human voice to create the Kabbalistic Divine Name of God encoded within the DNA of all life.

The Lost Chord. A sonic journey through the chakras and the Kabbalistic Tree of Life with sacred mantras, overtones, and mantric chanting from the Hindu, Tibetan, and Hebrew traditions, using frequencies and sacred ratios all employing the Fibonacci series. Runner-up: Best Healing and Meditation Album of the Year, 2000.

Medicine Buddha. This recording was created for His Holiness the Dalai Lama's teachings in Northern California of the "Heart of Wisdom" sutra and the "Medicine Buddha" initiation. Features the "Deep Voice" chanting of Tibetan chantmaster Lama Tashi, along with mantric choral voices, Tibetan singing bowls, Native American flute, guitar, and drums.

Trance Tara. An hour-long mantric chant to invoke Tara, Tibetan goddess of compassion and protection. It features male and female choral voices, Tibetan overtone chanting, singing bowls and bells, and tribal drumming. This recording has been featured in films and can be used for yoga, massage, dance, and tantric activity.

Music by Others

Due to the amount of music available, picking music that we use for enhancement of consciousness is difficult. This is not because we do not use such music but because we have favorites that we'll listen to for a while, change to something else, and then go back to listening to these. All those listed here are excellent, and we've also made sure that they're not out of print and are easily available.

Ambient 1: Music for Airports, by Brian Eno. This is dreamlike music played on synthesizers. Eno uses a few simple notes with organized variable loops to create deeply relaxing music that is great for meditation. It creates a beautiful atmosphere of sonic coloration, which seems to be felt more than heard. This recording has influenced many musicians.

Angels of the Deep, by Raphael. Raphael and his wife, Kutira, teach "Oceanic Tantra" in Hawaii. This beautiful album embodies this energy. It is a combination of celestial synthesizer sounds, coupled with harp, guitar, and flute, along with whale and ocean sounds. Wonderfully sensual and relaxing, this is a great recording for all sorts of tantric activity.

Chakra Suite, by Steven Halpern. Steven is one of the pioneers of healing music. This CD is one of the more influential and groundbreaking recordings, having influenced a whole generation of musicians. It is very slow pulsed, ambient keyboard music that is deeply calming and relaxing. It is a classic in its field.

Cho-Ku-Rei, by Weave. Weave is a gifted musician and weaver of sound who has created wonderful sonics on this album. Utilizing awareness of sound and sacred geometry, Weave has turned this Reiki symbol into a peaceful, soothing CD that is great for massage and healing. The music is slow, ambient, and very relaxing.

Hearing Solar Winds, by David Hykes and the Harmonic Choir. This music is beautiful and transformative. It features gorgeous choral voices creating vocal harmonics. Together Hykes and his choir build chords based on the harmonics in each other's tones and create Pythagorean tuned chords. The result is cloudlike in its sound and very hypnotic.

Rain of Blessing, by Lama Gyurme and Jean-Philippe Rykiel. Tibetan lama Gyurme unites with French composer Jean-Philippe Rykiel for an album of East meets West with delightful results. Combining the Tibetan monk's simple chant with New Age tingling bell synthesizer creates an ambience that is lovely and spiritual— helping the listener to embody compassion.

Tao of Healing, by Dean Evenson with Li Xiangting. Dean is a fine meditative flautist and Li Xiangting is a master on the *guqin,* an ancient seven-string zither from China. Together they create a slow and gentle recording. Supportive instrumentation includes keyboards, acoustic guitar, and percussion. This beautiful recording helps create a feeling of peace.

Thinking of You, by Kitaro. Kitaro is truly aware of the transforming power of sound. The music is beautiful—at times serene and other times majestic and uplifting. All of his albums are among our favorites and are highly recommended.

Appendix C

The Tantra of Sound Harmonizer

We created the recording *The Tantra of Sound Harmonizer* specifically as a sonic tool to generate balance and to bring harmony to individuals and couples. We believe it represents a new dimension of sound as a therapeutic and transformational modality. If people are already in harmony, the effects of this recording are extremely powerful. If listeners are out of harmony, *The Tantra of Sound Harmonizer* is even more useful and effective.

On this recording, we use sacred and scientific sound to make the most effective recording possible for assisting in personal development, healing, and consciousness acceleration. The CD incorporates chakra keynote frequencies, sacred vowels, *bija* mantras, Pythagorean tuning forks, and much more. The fusion of all these elements and effects, as well as the entrainment frequencies and chakra resonances, has never been done in this manner.

The recording works energetically both vertically and horizontally. Horizontally, it balances and aligns the chakras. Vertically, it synchronizes and balances the brain. This blend of different scientific and sacred sounds we've named Synchro-Sound because sounds are designed to assist in synchronizing a person to a state of balance, alignment, and wellness.

For those who wish maximum benefit from this recording, headphones are a must. The different entrainment frequencies, in particular, are most powerfully received using headphones. However, we have both enjoyed this recording using normal stereo CD players and found listening to it extremely helpful during the creation of this book.

Index

About the Authors

Jonathan Goldman, M.A., is an internationally renowned writer, musician, and teacher. He is an authority on sound healing and a pioneer in the field of harmonics. Jonathan is the author of *Healing Sounds, Shifting Frequencies,* and *The Lost Chord.* He has studied with masters of sound from both the scientific and spiritual traditions, incorporating this knowledge and energy into his teachings and healing music. His award-winning recordings include *Chakra Chants* and *The Lost Chord.* Jonathan is director of the Sound Healers Association in Boulder, Colorado, and CEO of Spirit Music. He teaches all over the world.

Andi Goldman, M.A., L.P.C., is a licensed psychotherapist, specializing in holistic counseling and sound therapy. She holds an M.A.

in counseling psychology from Boulder Graduate School and is Co-director of the Sound Healers Association and Director of the Healing Sounds Seminars. Andi is the developer of Tele-Counsel, the nation's first telephone counseling service specifically offering home-bound clients structured counseling. She has been an educator at international schools in Japan, Germany, and Indonesia and has lived and traveled extensively throughout the world. She is a musician, teacher, sound healer, and the wife and partner of Jonathan Goldman.

Together, Jonathan and Andi have dedicated their lives to the path of service, helping awaken and empower others with the ability of sound to heal and transform. They lecture and give workshops worldwide. They live in Boulder, Colorado, with their son and may be reached at: www.healingsounds.com, info@healingsounds.com, (303) 443-8181, or by writing to P.O. Box 2240, Boulder, CO 80306.

HAMPTON ROADS
PUBLISHING COMPANY, INC.

Now that you've read *Tantra of Sound,* we would like
to recommend other titles that will help you
explore your relationship with music, vibrations,
and those around you. We hope you will find these
additional titles interesting.

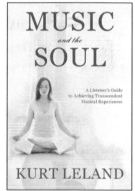

Music and the Soul
A Listener's Guide to Achieving
Transcendent Musical Experiences

Kurt Leland
Your guide to achieving transcendent musical experiences and a handbook on how music can increase your satisfaction and happiness in life.

ISBN 1-57174-367-7 · $16.95
6 x 9 Trade Paper · 432 pages

Soul Agreements

Dick Sutphen with Tara Sutphen
Your karmic road map was programmed at a soul level before you were born. Soul agreements established your relationships, career directions, and major challenges. Explore your destiny and learn how you can create your own reality.

ISBN 1-57174-442-8 · $14.95
5¹/₂ x 8¹/₂ Trade Paper · 192 pages
TO BE RELEASED MAY 2005

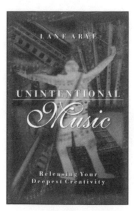

Unintentional Music
Releasing Your Deepest Creativity

Lane Arye

How to awaken your creativity using music as the starting point while including all art forms and ways of expression. Paying attention to unexpected events within the creative process will open the door to self-discovery.

ISBN 1-57174-260-3 · $13.95
5¹/₂ x 8¹/₂ TRADE PAPER · 248 PAGES

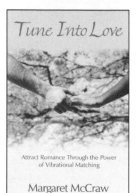

Tune into Love
Attract Romance through the Power of Vibrational Matching

Margaret McCraw

Using Vibrational Matching in her counseling practice, McCraw helps singles and couples find and maintain the relationship they desire. You will learn how to attract the partner of your dreams, and how to keep that relationship strong, loving, and vital.

ISBN 1-57174-430-4 · $14.95
5¹/₂ x 8¹/₂ TRADE PAPER · 256 PAGES
TO BE RELEASED JULY 2005

Naked Relationships
Sharing Your Authentic Self to Find the Partner of Your Dreams

Jan Denise

A smart, fun, and practical guide to building healthy, lasting relationships. This book offers sound advice on the physical, mental, and spiritual aspects of your love and life.

ISBN 1-57174-306-5 · $12.95
5 x 8 TRADE PAPER · 160 PAGES

Hampton Roads Publishing Company

. . . for the evolving human spirit

HAMPTON ROADS PUBLISHING COMPANY publishes books on a variety of subjects, including metaphysics, spirituality, health, visionary fiction, and other related topics.

We also create on-line courses and sponsor an *Applied Learning Series* of author workshops. For a current list of what is available, go to www.hrpub.com, or request the ALS workshop catalog at our toll-free number.

For a copy of our latest trade catalog, call toll-free, 800-766-8009, or send your name and address to:

HAMPTON ROADS PUBLISHING COMPANY, INC.
1125 STONEY RIDGE ROAD • CHARLOTTESVILLE, VA 22902
e-mail: hrpc@hrpub.com • www.hrpub.com

Recorded Examples for *Tantra of Sound*
Jonathan Goldman and Àndi Goldman

1. Introduction (3:15)

2. Taking a breath and releasing it with the *AH* sound (1:43)

3. Pronouncing the Vowel Sounds (5:06)

4. Experiencing the Vowel Sounds with pitches in the body (5:28)

5. Pronouncing the *Bija* Mantras (4:16)

6. Sounding the *Bija* Mantras on a monotone (3:15)

7. Sounding the Vowel Sounds on a major scale (11:33)

8. Sounding the Vowel Sounds on a monotone (4:00)

9. The *NURR* Sound (1:33)

10. The *MUAHZIDT* Sound (1:07)

11. The *VIZ* Sound (1:22)

12. The *HU* Sound (1:26)

13. The Vowels as Mantras Sound Bite in monotone (3:16)

14. The Vowels as Mantras Sound Bite in the major scale (2:36)

15. C and G Pythagorean Tuning Forks 2:3 (1:34)

16. DnA$^{\#}$ Tuning Forks 8:13 (1:16)

17. Crystal Bowl (2:44)

18. Tibetan Bowl (2:20)

19. *Ting Shas* (Tibetan Bells) (0:44)

20. Conclusion (1:50)

Total time (60:34)